WOO

MW00936054

THE LONG TREK

From the winding paths of Zululand
To the cobblestone streets of Prague

Real life stories from far away countries.

Dear Barbara,

May God get Honor and Glory
through this book of His leading
in my life,
Enjoy it! In Christ, Beverly

Beverly Pfeiffer Smith, R. N.

xulon PRESS

FOREWORD

§§§§

*A*nyone who has traveled overseas knows what an adventure that can be. This short story is about my experiences first as a single missionary, and then with my husband, Chuck.

Chuck and I met, courted, and married in South Africa. Our wedding took place where we later traveled so many dusty paths together, at Mosvold Mission Hospital and in the surrounding districts. This is not a fictional story, but one rich in everyday experiences of traveling the winding roads of Zululand. This trek eventually led to the cobblestone streets of Prague.

This book has been in the making for more than 20 years in my thoughts and intentions, and with others saying, "Bev, you should write a book."

My desire for the readers, and those who intend to be missionaries, is not to be overshadowed by the snake stories but to realize how God is truly active in one's life. All the honor and glory goes to the King of Kings!!

I wish to thank my husband, and all those who assisted and encouraged me in preparing **THE LONG TREK** for publication.

CONTENTS

Contents

Contents

BANG!

T he deafening sound of an explosion thundered through the neighborhood of 160 East 25th Street in Chicago Heights, Illinois. Fire engines, police, and an ambulance, with sirens screeching at high pitch, rushed to the scene. Immediately, people came out of their houses, and a crowd began to form. Among them was a 23-year old pregnant woman with two small children, one in her arms and the other clinging to her hand, as she ran to the scene. She knew that her husband was in that house, the home of his parents. She fought her way through the crowd, trying to get in the door, but the policemen refused her entrance.

The woman soon learned that her husband, Gus Tieri, had been experimenting with some chemicals thought to be a sulfuric compound. Since it was a hot summer day, the thought was that possibly a drop of perspiration fell onto the chemical, causing a violent reaction. He died soon after they had moved him from the basement up to the first floor of the house. Within a few hours of seeing her husband alive, Hazel found herself a widow with a five-year-old daughter, Elsie, a three-year-old son, Justin, and expecting another child. That child, Beverly, was born in late October.

I'm Beverly, and I came into the world at a difficult time for my mother. The following is an excerpt from the *Chicago Heights Star*:

GUS TIERI KILLED IN MYSTERIOUS BLAST:
Dies alone in Laboratory at Mother`s Home

The fatality which followed the late Sonny Talamont, Chicago Heights famed auto driver, in a racing career that ended in sudden death, extended last night to his closest associate, Gus Tieri, well known mechanical, metallurgist and chemist. Tieri was instantly killed at 10:25 o'clock in an explosion at the home of his mother, 160 East Twenty-Fifth Street.

For many months Tieri had spent a large share of his spare time in the basement of his mother's home. There he had rigged out an impromptu laboratory, and there he worked numerous experiments with powerful chemicals. The eventual object of his work was not known, for almost always he was in the basement alone, locking himself in and remaining often until a late hour at night.

Last night he had followed his usual custom and was alone in the basement when the house was shaken by a terrific explosion. Relatives on the first floor rushed below to find Tieri's mangled body lying in the midst of wrecked equipment and furnishings. His right arm and his legs were blown literally to bits. A large curved slug of steel, like a piece of shrapnel, had pierced his heart.

The explosion attracted a large number of people to the scene, many of whom had been friends of the dead man. Soon scores of people were clustered about the front porch and in the hallway, all attempting to push their way to the basement. One boy, Raymond Palanca, of 223 East Twenty-First Street, was painfully injured when a railing on the front porch collapsed, and he fell to the ground. *He was taken to the police station for emergency treatment and was later sent home. Police arrived at the house in time to keep order among the crowd.*

The body was removed to an undertaking establishment, and an inquest was set for two o'clock this afternoon. Elaborate funeral arrangements will probably be completed sometime today. Tieri was employed at the time of his death, it was stated, at the Victor Chemical plant.

He had formerly held a position at the Columbia Tool Steel company, and was an expert mechanic. He was Sonny Talamont`s mechanical when the latter was at the top of his fame and burning up dirt tracks with the speedy little racer on which he and Tieri worked. Tieri was 28 years old. He was married and lived at 163 East Twenty-Third Street. In addition to the wife, a three year old son and a five year old daughter survive. He had many friends in all parts of the city.

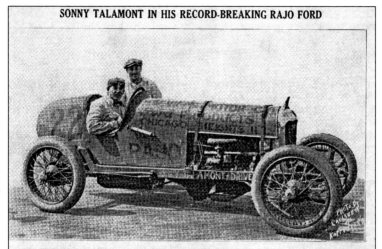

SONNY TALAMONT IN HIS RECORD-BREAKING RAJO FORD

THIS IS THE RACING OUTFIT THAT HAS GIVEN CHICAGO HEIGHTS TOP NOTCH RECOGNITION ON THE FASTEST DIRT TRACKS IN THE COUNTRY. IN THIS CAR SONNY SET A NEW MARK OF .47 FLAT FOR THE MILE ROBY TRACK, WHICH WAS CONSIDERED THE MOST REMARKABLE PERFORMANCE EVER RECORDED ON A MILE DIRT TRACK. THE CAR, WHICH IS A RAJO FORD, HAS PROVEN TO BE THE FASTEST FORD RACER EVER BUILT. IN FACT SONNY FAR OUTSTRIPS EVEN THE 300 CUBIC INCH FRONTENACS. EVERY PART OF WHICH IS BUILT ESPECIALLY FOR RACING. WITH SONNY IN THE PICTURE IS GUS TIERI, FAITHFUL MECHANICIAN, WHO HAS BEEN A REAL FACTOR IN TALAMONT'S SUCCESS.

My father standing by the racer

Gus Tieri is pictured here with Sonny Talamont and his racing "Rajo." Sonny was killed in a racing accident in July 1927.

From an article in the Crown Point, Indiana, newspaper of July 18, we read:

Sonny Talamont, 28, of Chicago Heights, one of the leading dirt track automobile racers in the Middle West, was killed in a smash-up in the five-mile event of the

American Legion racing program here today. Talamont, with nine other drivers, had just been flagged down by the officials, who ruled the start illegal, and was in the second lap of the event on the one-half mile track. His car skidded, reeled and lunged into the air, throwing Talamont from his seat to the track. Another car struck him, killing him instantly, and crashed into his wrecked machine. In the jam that followed Billy Arnold of Chicago was seriously injured. The field was going approximately sixty miles an hour when the accident occurred. Six thousand persons witnessed the crash.

PART ONE

1

Profile Of The Author

My Birth

I made my entrance into this world as Beverly Jean, at St. James Hospital in Chicago Heights. My weight was 5 pounds, 13 ounces at birth. However, I didn't gain enough weight after being home, so I was taken back to the hospital on Friday night in late January. That hospital stay lasted until February 18, a total of three weeks and three days. My weight upon entering the hospital was 6 pounds, 2 ounces, but with the good care and a special formula, I was able to go home weighing 7 pounds, 12 ounces — at nearly four months old.

At the bottom of my baby's record is this saying:

He who builds well in the life of a child builds a monu-
ment reaching toward the sky and sets in motion a ripple
on the Sea of Purpose. . . a force and influence for good
that goes on and on in expanding circles to cease only on
the shores of a boundless eternity.

Little did this newborn know to what extent some of this would become reality for her in the years ahead.

Early Childhood

Sometime after my birth, and within the next two years, my mother and her three children moved from Chicago Heights, Illinois, to Grand Rapids, Michigan, near an aunt. She purchased a large house, with an upstairs apartment on Briggs Street in the North Park area. Sometimes we would live downstairs and rent out the upstairs, and at other times, we would live upstairs and rent out the larger downstairs apartment. During this time, my brother was born. We lived there until I was in the second grade. The Depression still had its effect on the economy, and my mother lost the house.

Eventually, she remarried. Then after my sister was born, we moved to a house on Effie Street, also in North Park. A year later we moved again, across the street. During those two years, my mother, as well as some of us children were terribly abused in many ways, so she divorced. Partly because of that, and for financial reasons, we moved to a small upstairs apartment on California Avenue, on the northwest side of Grand Rapids. I attended the fifth and sixth grades at the Lexington School. With no father, I remember times when I would see an older, gentle-looking man and think to myself, "Oh, he would be a nice father." I longed for a nice father.

The next year, we moved to the northeast side of Grand Rapids on Sweet Street, where I attended seventh grade at Creston High. A year later, we moved back to the west side on Straight Street, where I completed my eighth and ninth grades at Union High. During this time, my mother met and married the most terrific man I had always dreamed about having as a father. He adopted the three younger children, who were underage. I was the eldest of the three.

Since my new father came from Rockford, Michigan, he and my mother decided to buy an old farmhouse on 40 acres northeast of Rockford. I had six weeks until I was done with ninth grade at Union High, so during the week, I boarded with my Sunday school teacher, Lucielle Reigersberg, and took the bus over to Union High. I would go home to Rockford on the weekends. My tenth grade began at Rockford High with my newly adopted surname, Pfeiffer, and I graduated in 1946. This is my physical background. Now I'd would like to share with you spiritual background.

Spiritual background

Even as a five-year-old, I had a desire to go to church, and often went alone to Sunday school. I heard about Jesus and cherished the weekly Sunday school leaflets, and especially the picture of Jesus surrounded by children. Also, I would have a guilty conscience toward God if I did something wrong, like telling lies, cheating when playing with other kids, etc.

I still had fun with others, and was more of a tomboy. I would climb trees, stomp my shoes into empty tin cans and run down the alley in the back of our house, just making noise. I would curl up and get inside the rim of an old tire and be rolled down the alley, etc.

When we moved to Effie Street, we lived across from a retired lady who had been a missionary in China. It was in that period of time that a radio program was broadcast that dramatized the end of the world. Everyone seemed so concerned, but this lady assured my mother, that according to the Bible, that was not how the world would end.

I still was not going to a church, but just having fun growing up. The street we lived on was a hill. In the wintertime, all the neighborhood kids and even some adults would sled down the whole block and still glide to the end of the next block. There were also times when the police would block off the street intersecting our street. As I reflect on those times, I marvel that God was protecting me from real danger. Sometimes we would go two on a sled, piggyback style, much faster. Instead of going straight at the end of the hill, we would go under a small pipe-type fence, which was only about two feet high. If I had raised my head, I'm sure that the pipe would have struck me square in the forehead — probably splitting open my skull!

Also, at the end of the two blocks was a creek with a water wheel. We would always go to school by taking that shortcut, but we would have to jump the creek. It was easier to jump it on our way to school, because the bank was higher

25

on that side. However, coming home meant jumping from the lower bank to the upper bank. We didn't always succeed, which meant wet clothes. Also, this way to and from school meant going through woods, in which veterans from the Soldiers' Home would often walk. If I was alone, I would be afraid, and I would run all the way through the woods.

When we moved to the west side of Grand Rapids, there were six of us in a two-bedroom apartment. We were still very poor, but we had a large chestnut tree in our back yard. In the fall, we collected the nuts, still green, and my mother would throw them into the pot-bellied stove, which heated the apartment. There was much enjoyment for us kids in hearing the loud bangs as they broke their shells and hit against the sides of the stove. However, the people living downstairs were rather annoyed, so we stopped that!

Many times we went to bed with only milk poured over a piece of bread for our supper. When our shoes would wear through, my mother would take thick cardboard and put it inside the shoe. Our Christmases were brightened by the gifts from the "Santa Claus Girls," a charitable organization.

I marvel at God's provision through all those years, up to the time of my mother's last marriage. She did all she could by taking in washing and ironing, cleaning at the school, and walking into downtown Grand Rapids for shopping to avoid paying the bus fare. My brother sold magazines each week, until he started laying down his magazine bag and going off to play. This meant that my mother would have to pay for those magazines not sold.

As a young eight year old, I would often look up to heaven, and think that when I died I wanted to go there, but I didn't know how. I had a definite sense of God, but never really knew Him.

Across from my Lexington school was a church. I often wanted to go there, but was too timid to ask my mother. None of my family ever went to church. Finally, I did ask. She gave me permission, and I went. It was a Sunday when they served communion, and I took it. I had no understanding of what I had done. I had such a longing to please God that I thought I had done something wrong by drinking "wine." When I told my mother about the incident, I was crying, and she just knowingly laughed at me. However, in my heart I was still searching for the way to heaven.

When I walked in downtown Grand Rapids, I would pass a store which had an open Bible in the window and a sign that read, "Come in and inquire more." I often considered that someday I would go in. Much later, I realized the organization behind that storefront was a cult. Then, too, on my way to school, I had to pass a church where I would see the nuns meditating as they walked around their premises. I would think, "If anyone is holy and going to heaven, they must be. I'll be a nun when I grow up." I still marvel at His grace and keeping power until He led me to Himself, as the Way, the Truth, and the Life.

When we moved to the northeast side of Grand Rapids, and I was in Creston High School, we lived just off Plainfield Avenue, right behind an ice cream establishment. At the end of the street was a church with steps going up to a large cement platform in front of the edifice itself. As kids, we would often go there to roller skate on the smooth cement. One day, the pastor was changing the notice board. I thought he would chase us away, but he just spoke kindly to us and let us keep on skating there. Little did I know what an influence the pastor, Rev. Keithly, and this church would have on me later in life.

New Life in Christ

One day my girlfriend Violet, who lived behind me, said, "Hey, Bev, they're having Daily Vacation Bible School down at the church. Let's go." So I said, "O. K." We went, and a missionary lady from South America taught us the whole two weeks. I do not remember what she taught, but on the last day after class was dismissed, I went to her with tears streaming down my face. I don't know what I said, but she knew what I was seeking. My girlfriend and I both met with the pastor. I didn't know what was happening, except I knew I was very sinful before God.

From that time on, I began to go to church. I enjoyed the more informal evening service with a lot of singing. Being very short for my age, I would sit right in the front row. I wanted to learn all I could about God, even amidst all my tears, mostly out of concern for my mother. Two weeks after my redemption from sin, a missionary spoke in the evening service, and I told the Lord that I would be willing to go to China as a missionary. I was in the seventh grade then.

My attendance at Sunday school became regular from that point. My teacher was a single lady who taught with sincerity of heart. I would read my Bible upstairs at night-time by the light of a five watt bulb. Between Sunday school and the morning service, my teacher, Lucielle, would stay those 15 minutes with me to answer my questions. She could have dismissed the class and gone to fellowship with her friends during that time, but she never refused time for me. She would even let me sit with her and her family during the morning service. I also started to go to the mid-week prayer service, attended by all adults, but she would be there with me. I didn't pray out loud for a long time, but when I did, it was very hard for me to even say the name of Jesus, because I had heard it all my life in a cursing connotation. I kept going to church and Sunday school and to the evening service until my mother said I was getting too "religious." From then on, I could only go once on Sunday, so I chose the Sunday school, because I could ask Lucielle any questions I had, and then slip out the back door of the church before the service commenced.

As much as I wanted to have my mother saved, I could never tell her how. I would just shed tears when I asked her if she was going to heaven. However, one time when Lucielle asked her if she saw any change in me, she replied, "Yes, she seems more appreciative." So even though sensing the seriousness of my mother's need of salvation, I could not tell her what had happened to me. In fact, I didn't even know what had really happened to me. However, I knew I had found the way to heaven, and I know He offers eternal life to all who come to Him. Another event in my spiritual growth was the girls' group of AWANA — "Approved Workmen Are Not Ashamed." AWANA was held at the church on Thursday evenings. This helped me to grow spiritually. I was allowed to go to that. However, when we moved to the west side of Grand Rapids, I wondered how I would ever get to church. Then another girl's grandparents would pick me up on Sunday mornings. I never knew if they would come or not, but I always got up, dressed, and sat on the bottom of the upstairs steps by the window to watch for them, while the rest of the household would still be sleeping.

I deeply anticipated going to church on Sunday mornings, but I really wanted to go to AWANA on Thursday evenings. When I asked my mother, she said I could go. I went, even though I walked the four miles to and four miles back across Grand Rapids, from the northwest side to the northeast side. Just occasionally, she would give me the five-cent bus fare. It was during World War II, and there were many soldiers stationed in downtown Grand Rapids. I had to walk past blocks of dark factory buildings along dimly lighted streets, both there and in my neighborhood. If I looked back and saw a man even several yards behind me, I would run far ahead. Even through these times, I would see God's protection. At times I was scared, yes, but determined to learn all I could about my Lord.

There were times that my mother would say, "You cannot go next week." But the next week, I would get ready, and since she didn't say I could not go, I would go. I would not disobey her, but she never said I could not go that night, nor did she stop me.

It was strange, but true, that I never had homework on Thursday evenings. She would ask me why I never had homework on Thursday, and I just never did. AWANA was His provision for me to go to a Bible camp. I earned that for attendance, memorizing Bible verses, etc. There, I was with other believers for a whole two week period. That spurred me on to a deeper knowledge and thankfulness for my salvation.

His Plan for My Life

Now back to my seventh-grade vow of going to the mission field.

I began to realize that in order to become a missionary, I would have to go to college. Since we were poor, I thought that it would be impossible. Therefore, in high school I began the commercial course instead of the college course. However, God kept reminding me of my vow. I knew I had to trust God, but I was not fully committed to that trust. So in my sophomore year, I took half commercial and half college-prep courses. In my junior year, I switched completely over to college-prep courses, which meant that I had to take five solids, instead of the normal four, to make up all the required credits I would need to graduate. We lived out in the country, and I still had a lot of "chores" and housework to do, so often I would only begin my homework between 7 and 9 pm., and would finish late. Still, the Lord kept the burden of the lost before me — especially my family and my grandmother, whom I loved dearly.

While we still lived in Grand Rapids, I had earned enough points in AWANA to go to camp in the summer, but since we had just moved to the country and gotten started into part-time farming (my father worked daily at the shoe factory in Rockford), my mother said that I could not go. There was just too much work to be done. Before we moved from the city, I wondered why the Lord was taking me away from church. I thought that I would not get to church in Rockford, and it was true. I was allowed to go on Christmas and Easter, with my dad taking me by car and picking me up. Times when there was no pressing field or house work, I was allowed to walk the eight-mile round trip. I was so thrilled that I didn't consider it a hardship — one time even in wintry, blizzard-like conditions.

I tried not to use any restrictions as an excuse, but I was concerned about working on Sundays. Once when I asked my mother if I could go to church the next day, she replied, "No, there's too much work. If you don't work, you don't eat." I respected her, and felt I had cleared myself before God by not disobeying her. So I went out to drag the plowed field before we planted corn, and with the loud, old Fordson tractor, I sang to my Lord at the top of my lungs. I came to enjoy country living as it afforded me a quiet place to learn from my Master Himself.

After High School

It was the summer of my high school graduation when my mother went to the mailbox and found a postcard from Lucielle congratulating me. She wrote, "What do you plan now? Moody Bible Institute?" When my mother read that, she said, "You know, Bev, they could send you as a missionary." I remember that she was canning, and she went to the basement to get more jars. When she came up, the first thing she said was, "Bev, you know, they could send you to China." I replied, "That's where I want to go." So my intentions were well-known to her.

After high school graduation, I went to work at the shoe factory where my dad worked. My job was sewing tongues onto work shoes. Most of the women were on piece work, but I could never get up to their speed. Also, since I was so much shorter, it was hard for me to get the heavy wooden boxes off the conveyer belt. The machines were large, so my back and arms would ache at the end of the day. I was paid $21 a week, but by the time deductions were made, I had $19.50 left. We got paid Friday mornings. At lunchtime, I would go immediately to the bank to deposit $15 toward college. I paid $3 a week to my mother for room and board, and kept the $1.50 for incidentals. However, I detested my job, so after five months, I quit and went to Grand Rapids in search of a secretarial job. Since I had very little money, I walked long distances to answer want ads, but to no avail. After several days of no success, I went back home and asked for a job back at the same factory. This time they gave me a better job: splitting horse hide with another employee.

It was so much easier; a deafening noise, but easier physically, even though I stood all day.

One evening I was talking with a friend, Ione, who was still in high school, and I asked her what she was going to do after graduation. She said she was going to college for a year to get pre-med for nursing. The thought just came to me that that would be good for the mission field.

I had always wanted to be a teacher. I loved and was active in sports, and had thought that sports and teaching could be used in missions. My mother had only once said to me that I would be a good nurse, but I had dismissed that because I would gag if I even got near someone who was vomiting. So it surprised me that I would even consider nursing as a possibility now. However, it began to be more prominent in my thoughts, so I began to search for colleges that would serve me in this area. My mother hoped that I would go to a college near home. Then, a girl gave me a yearbook from a college in the south. I liked what I saw, but had no intention of going that far away. So I teasingly said to the Lord, "You are going to have to have Mom say yes."

As it happened, that night, I said, "Mom, what do you think about me going to South Carolina to college?" Her reply stunned me. "Well, Bev, it's your money," she said. "If you want to go, it's up to you." I took that to be a sign from the Lord that that was His will for me, and I went.

Nurses' Training

After a year and a half of college, my money was running out, so I decided to apply to a nursing school in Chicago, where my friend had gone. Even though (on my mother's advice) I had informed them that I was only 4'8" tall. The reply came back that as long as I was strong and healthy, I would be accepted.

So in September of 1949, I rode a Greyhound bus to the big city of Chicago, where my friend met me at Union Station and took me to Swedish Covenant Hospital. The tuition I paid left me with very little savings, and we understood that we would not receive any stipend (except for free room and board) for the three years of training. I had to continue to learn to trust my Provider, not just for finances, but for wisdom to follow Him whatever the circumstances.

There were many times I had to trust Him to MAKE me a nurse. We had five months of probation to see if we were academically qualified to stay in training. When that time came, we "probies" were called in one-by-one to notify us of

37

our fate. During that time, I kept saying to the Lord, "Lord, I KNOW you want me to be a missionary nurse." I knew that my grades on tests were only mediocre, although my practical work was satisfactory, and my heart would skip a beat every time I heard that someone had been sent home. Finally, my turn came, and as I stood before the Director of Nurses, my heart was beating like a big drum. When I heard her say, "You may stay — on probation," I knew, more than ever, that He wanted me to be a missionary nurse. I knew that I still had to work hard, which I did. Some of my classmates would quiz me the night before a test and were satisfied that I knew the material well, but the test results would come back just above passing.

Once during my affiliation at Children's Memorial Hospital for pediatrics, the director called me into her office. She said that my practical work was good, but my written work was not. She told me, "The doctors give you high recommendations, which they do not usually do, but you do not do well on your written tests. Why is that?" I just stood there and said, "I don't know." (This had been my story all through my education. I guess I would just freeze up when it came to tests.) Apparently, they were willing to overlook that failing; at the end of my affiliation, the director wrote on my report, "She would make a good pediatric head nurse." That gave me great encouragement from my Lord. All through my training, I would remind God that He called me to be a missionary nurse, and HE would have to get me through.

We had a tremendous nurses' class, women who stuck together. First, we were "probies" who wore a striped uniform with a white apron for five months. Then, if our grades and practical work were up to par, we were given a white bib to go with the apron. Also, we were "capped" in a lovely candlelight ceremony. We really wore our uniforms with great pride.

We all have great memories of some of our patients, like Granny Ferry, a long-term resident. After bathing her, we would have to get her up into a chair, which entailed 4-5 nurses. She was not only very heavy, but also *very* uncooperative. A derrick would have been a huge asset!

Then there was a petite old lady who was always climbing over the side rails. One day after I had completed her bath, I was putting up the side rails, and she looked up at me with pitiful eyes and said, "Oh, Dearie, please don't put up those rails. They're *so* hard to climb over!"

Another time as I was bathing a man who was hallucinating, he said, "Do you see those men on the wall over there?" Realizing his condition and hurriedly trying to get my assignments done, I just agreed, "Yeah. Yeah." His reply caught me up short when he said, "No, you don't. You're not even looking!" And I wasn't!

There were also times of weariness and discouragement. Sometimes we would gather in the "utility" room and lay out our complaints to one another for consolation. One in our class was always quoting poems, etc. Dear June "Willy" Williams would come in quoting, "Have you come to the Red Sea place in your life, where you can't go around, or you can't go back? You have to go through." That would be enough to stop our complaining and spur us on.

I will ever be so thankful that I was allowed to become a nurse. I still love nursing, the study of medicine, and helping people. And what a great opportunity to tell them about Jesus!

2

The Trek Begins

Preparation

*A*fter graduating from nursing, I went back home and lived with my parents, while working at Butterworth Hospital in Grand Rapids. Also, for the second half of the school year, I enrolled in the evening school at the local Baptist Bible Institute. In the fall, I enrolled full time in the day school and worked nights at the hospital. I took 18-19 credit hours, but I had to cut down my hospital commitment to 32 hours' night duty. I needed the money to pay for my tuition and books, as well as my room and board, and gas to run my car. I never had any "extra."

I still helped with the AWANA club at church, and loaded my little two-door Chevy with kids who would not have been able to attend. Recently, after 50 years, I met a lady in the grocery store, who recognized me as the one who used to pick her up and take her to AWANA. It is amazing how God will bring across our paths those whom we have unknowingly helped in their walk with God.

I wanted to learn all I could about the Bible, so in my last year at the Bible school, I took 19 hours. There was only one hour left, and so I filled it in with Bible Geography. This was God's leading, because in the middle of the school year I learned that I had enough credits to graduate, but Bible Geography was one of the requirements. I wanted so much to go to the mission field as soon as God would allow me, so I completed my Bible requirements in two years instead of the normal three.

I had already been accepted with T.E.A.M. (The Evangelical Alliance Mission) when I became acquainted with another very Godly missionary from another African country. They needed a nurse desperately. This caused confusion as to where God wanted me. I didn't want to be out of His will. I even traveled to one of their mission conferences to see if that was the right one for me. I remember standing in the back of the auditorium and hearing God whispering to me, "This is not for you," even though the other mission was a highly respected one. I struggled with that decision, but every time I almost withdrew my T.E.A.M. application, seemingly for no reason I would receive a letter from the director of T.E.A.M, Dr. Mortenson, just wanting to know how I was doing. Then, I would think, "How can I leave this Mission?" I went back and forth on this for about three months, and finally decided on T.E.A.M. Then I had no more doubts. After a time in South Africa, I was so glad it was final. I could have been in Africa, where I knew God wanted me. I could have been doing nursing, for which I had trained. I could have been in a good mission, with which I was acquainted. All this could have been, BUT I could have been out of God's will. When times got rough in South Africa, and I would wonder if I was in the right place, I could always go back to how God led, and it would be settled.

After graduation, I worked full time on the 11:00-7:00 hospital shift and began "deputation" (the act of a deputy or person to represent others). This entailed going to different churches by invitation to give my testimony of salvation and to express my desire to serve my Lord in South Africa at the Mosvold Mission Hospital at Ingwavuma, Zululand.

The response of the congregation was to stand behind me in prayer and financial support, with the first item being my priority. I really enjoyed meeting with the people and thoroughly enjoyed sharing what God had done and was doing in my life. I became impatient, though, and it seemed like an eternity before I had all the backing that was required. Finally, I met all my medical and other requirements and was given the okay to book my flight. I knew, and accepted, the fact that by faith in God, I would receive $50.00 a month, and be paid every three months. At that time, 1956, the exchange rate in S.A. gave me the equivalent of $35.00 USD a month. After furlough, it was raised a little.

Off to South Africa

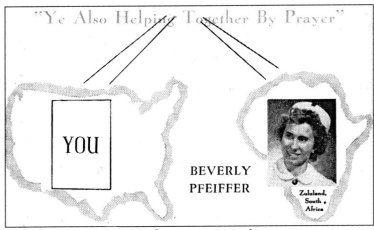

"Ye Also Helping Together By Prayer"

YOU

BEVERLY
PFEIFFER

Zululand,
South
Africa

My first prayer card

I left Grand Rapids, Michigan, on April 19, 1956 — just nine months after I began the deputation process. (Now over 50 years later, some desiring missionaries are delayed from two to three years.) I was the first missionary in our mission to fly to South Africa. One of the nurses there was so overworked they thought she might be heading for a stroke, so they wanted me there in a hurry. I arrived in Johannesburg on April 21, 1956; I was just naive enough to trust the Lord that I didn't even think about anyone meeting me.

While we were flying, one of the stewardesses noticed I was reading my Bible. She in turn mentioned it to the pilot, who was a believer. On his break he came back, sat next to me, and we had a good conversation. He was planning to stay a few days with some other missionaries in Johannesburg (Jo'burg), and when he asked me if someone was meeting me, I had to admit that I didn't know. He said if I got stuck, he would help. So you see that God always has someone in your path to help you if you need it. He never leaves you alone. As it turned out, Marlin and Gladys Olsons, who worked in Jo'burg, brought Ruth Aronson, a nurse from the hospital, to the airport to meet me. As I climbed the stairs, I can still remember the joy of seeing them leaning over the rail and calling to me. I had arrived!! Later, I found out that the intended message of someone meeting me never reached me.

We stayed with the Olsons a couple of days, before we boarded the train for Zululand! One of the first words I picked up in Jo'burg was the word "shame." It is a word that can be used to express almost any emotion, just by different intonations. You could say "Oh, shame!" to a person who dropped something, or to someone who made a mistake, or a wrong turn in the road, or to show your delight in a baby, a small child, or even a puppy. When I first heard it, I thought, I'll never say THAT!" Before we were halfway to Zululand, I found myself saying, "Oh, shame!" to almost everything.

Dr. and Mrs. Taylor met us at the small town of Piet Retief and took us the rest of the way to the Mosvold Mission Hospital at Ingwavuma, on top of the 200-mile-long Ubombo Mountain range. Ubombo, in Zulu, means "rib"; thus, the range is in the shape of a rib. It was dark when we drove through the hospital gate. My heart was throbbing with excitement. As I emerged from the car, I heard the whispering wind blowing through the tall eucalyptus trees, and the sound reminded me of the same scenario at our home back in Rockford. I LOVED it!! I was HOME! Everyone came out to greet us, and it made me praise God that after all those years of preparations, and in His timing, He brought me to where He had planned long ago. In my heart, I could not stop praising Him for His faithfulness.

Little did I know that, except for clinic trips in the low veldt, I would be off this mountain only twice in my five-and-a-half-year term. Maybe it would have been nice to have gone more often, but I was very content.

Mosvold Mission Hospital

There were three of us *"Amas"* (Zulu nickname for *Amakhosazana*, which meant an unmarried lady) living in the same house. Then two others would join us for meals. They were gracious enough to let me have a month to adjust before my turn of a week of cooking. We did have an African lady who actually did the cooking, but we had to put the food out for her and instruct her. We would make our own breakfasts, because we all had different schedules. We all shared the expenses. At times it was trying, because one person didn't like liver, another one could not eat something else, and so it went. But we all managed somehow to maintain our strength. The main meal was at noon, and we ate lighter in the evening. Our week of cooking also included ordering vegetables, which came 200 miles from Durban, on a train to Gollela, 30 miles away at the bottom of the mountain, Then, the "lorry" — a five-ton open truck — would go to bring it up the winding, dusty road to the hospital.

At the time, our bread, unsliced white or brown and unwrapped, would be delivered to the country store in the village, on top of the passenger bus three times a week. The loaves were in a gunny sack and thrown off the top of the bus onto the bare, dusty ground. Sometimes the bag would break open and the loaves would fall out on the dirt road. It would be picked up and placed back in the bag and sold. And we all survived!!!

Mosvold Mission Hospital was a hospital with a school of nursing. African girls would apply and according to their level of schooling and their recommendations, would be accepted. Usually we would only be able to accept maybe 12 to 14 girls out of about 70. Most of them only had our equivalent of a sixth- to eighth-grade education. They also had to be able to speak English, because all of their government requirements and exams were done in that vernacular. They were taught everything the same as an R.N. in the States. When the hospital first opened in 1952, the nurses had to be taught how to use a door stop, a telephone, and even to turn on a faucet. These were not a part of their lives living in a mud hut.

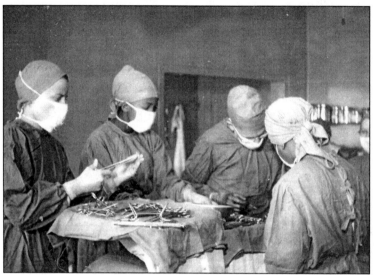

An operation in progress

I was assigned to teach the African nurses in the department of surgery. They had to learn sterile technique, scrubbing in for surgeries, packing drape bundles, preparing things for autoclaving, etc. Also there was the selecting of the necessary instruments needed for the upcoming surgery, and boiling them in water over two kerosene burners. It also meant making up different draping packs for the different types of surgeries and seeing that they got autoclaved. We had to be prepared for any type of surgery-a cesarean section, a hernia, a crocodile bite, a human bite, a stab wound, a ruptured spleen, broken bones, and skin grafting from burns. This was especially true for very young children, who during their sleep, would roll into the small fire that burned in the middle of the hut.

We always had Tuesdays for scheduled surgeries, but emergencies had no schedule. One night we had three emergency C-sections, and I told Doc that we didn't have any more sterile bundles to do another one. I went home to bed, and wouldn't you know it!! An hour later, I got called out for another C-section. We had to take several minor packs to get enough to make a major pack for sterile draping for that operation. God is good <u>ALL</u> the time, and He gave much wisdom and strength.

To be called out at night meant for two nurses with a lighted Coleman lantern to come to my bedroom window, and tap on it to wake me up. I then would dress and go up to the hospital. I usually had batteries for my "torch" (flashlight), but occasionally, for one reason or another, I didn't have a new supply, and I would walk up to the hospital by feeling the worn path under my feet. I was always thinking of the possibility of stepping on a snake. They were prevalent, but God protected me. I was especially concerned about the boom-slang snake that was seen in the huge tree under whose large branches I had to pass. This is a most deadly snake, which causes internal bleeding, even of the organs. It usually causes death within 20 minutes.

When the moon shines in Africa, one can see the beauty of the night, with the stars sparkling ever so brightly, but when it is not, it is really pitch black. On a beautiful full moon, we single girls would say, "Africa a land of wasted moonlight!" Being on the top of the mountain, we could see the light of the fires in the *kraals*, or grass huts, down in the low veldt. Some were glowing brightly, and others dimly. I often wondered if the light of my life was shining so that others could see it clearly. God taught me many lessons, and I failed Him so many times, yet He kept me going.

Arial view of hospital

Nurses graduation

The hospital was so situated on the top of the mountain that when we came from the low veldt clinic on Friday nights, we could see the lights of the various buildings all in a row. It looked like a train. "A city built on a hill cannot be hid." We wanted it to be a vibrant testimony. "Mosvold Mission Hospital— that men might know the love of God" was the sign on the Outpatient wall. And even though the South African government has taken over the hospital, the brass sign is still there, as well as some Christian doctors and African nurses. The testimony continues!

I was also given the responsibility of the pharmacy, which entailed filling the wards' medicine bottles, and ordering all the medicines from the various drug warehouses. This need had to be anticipated three to four months in advance to allow for the shipment by train from long distances. It also meant pricing the medicine for charging the patients. It was remarkable how so many patients would come back month after month and pay a "ticky" (less than 3 cents) on their bill until it was all paid. Usually their bills were equivalent to about one to two dollars.

Another responsibility I was given was the "European" outpatient department. Under the apartheid authority, we had to have a separate examining room for the white race. Most of these people were government employees from the nearby village. There were not many who came, but the visits were never scheduled, so I would have to leave other things in order to care for them. If I were busy in surgery, another nurse would cover for me.

One 14-year-old boy tried to commit suicide and had to be flown to the large government hospital in Durban. Since I was the smallest and lightest nurse, I was allocated to travel in the small two-seater plane, and to hold the intravenous bottle above him. We had some rough weather, so it was not easy to hold the bottle high *and* to control him. I was glad when we landed in Durban.

All these responsibilities usually required a 14-to-16-hour day. All four of us "sisters" (a nomenclature recognized by the South African government for an R.N. in the States) and the two doctors worked long hours. After about a year, we decided that we all should have a regularly scheduled day off, and one person would cover for the other, which also included night call. This was a big help. Then when one of the sisters went on furlough, it was decided that I should also take all the night surgery calls. Often I would be up during the night, but still had to work the next day. One night I was so tired that when the staff nurses tapped on my window, I fell back to sleep and woke up an hour later and went up to the hospital. The next morning in report she read, "Sister Pfeiffer was called at 2:30 a.m., and responded at 3:30 a.m." I was embarrassed, but so thankful that God woke me up even an hour later.

Many times we had patients come in because of fighting and stabbing. One woman needed an emergency operation because she had been stabbed with an object like an ice pick directly into her heart. It came within a quarter of an inch of her aorta valve. Her friends had stuffed semidry leaves into the hole to stop the bleeding. We operated, and she lived!!!

Another incident happened when two women were fighting, and one bit into the lower lip of the other person. With other injuries, we had to admit them both in the same ward — next to each other in the only beds we had empty. We only had room for 12 beds in a ward, so we often had to put the ones who needed the least attention on a grass mat on the floor between the beds. Since they usually didn't have beds in their huts, they often requested to lie on a mat on the floor. This eliminated the fear of falling out of a bed.

Our pediatric ward was almost always overcrowded with children who had severe kwashiorkor (a condition of sunken eyes, a distended abdomen, wiry reddish hair and very lethargic), or were dehydrated, had burns, dysentery, and even tetanus. One little boy, Malinjojo, was very sick. During the nurses' midnight rounds, he was awake. They asked him if he needed anything, or if he was in pain. He just said, "No." Then he asked the nurse, "Does Jesus love a boy like me?" She was able to reassure him about Jesus' love, and then continued on with her rounds. When she came back for the 3-a.m. rounds, she found that little Malinjojo had died. We knew Jesus had taken him into His own arms.

Some incidents were not so pleasant. One child died in the late evening. The mother insisted on taking the child home for the burial the next day. We tried to convince her to wait until daylight, but we had to let her go. It was heartbreaking to see her strap the dead eight-year-old child on her back, and step out barefoot into the dark night to walk the long distance down the mountain. Had we failed to give her the hope there is in Christ?

Ready for clinic trip

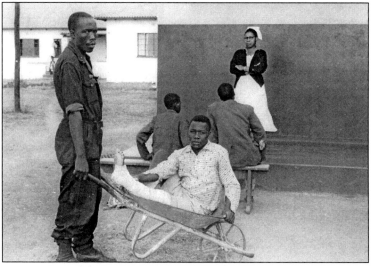

Friendly transportation

Our "ambulance" was a pickup truck. The Africans had no telephones, and the village phone was active during the day only from 8 a.m. to 5 p.m., with a lunch break from 12 to 1 p.m., a half-day on Saturday, and off all day Sunday. So if someone needed an ambulance, a friend or relative had to walk the many miles, or pass word along, to notify the hospital nurses. Sometimes it was a woman in difficult labor, or a crocodile bite victim, a broken leg, a snake bite, etc. Sometimes they would transport the patient in a wheelbarrow, even on a donkey, or in anything available.

However, one emergency call concerned a young girl. The missionary ambulance driver took the informer with him for directions to the *kraal* (the family home), which consisted of several grass thatched huts. One hut was for the parents, one for the girls, one for the boys, one for the kitchen, and one for entertaining. There are no streets, signs, or addresses.

They got to the *kraal* and found the girl's leg all wrapped up with cloths, so they put her in the back of the pickup. There were a few more stops on the way, but when they reached the hospital they were amazed at the seriousness of the wounds the crocodile had inflicted. Yet, all the time she rode in the back of the truck over stony, and bumpy roads — even paths — she never once cried out with all her pain.

Another time a lady was brought to us with a ruptured spleen. While trying to gather a few figs from a tree for her family, she had fallen out. We had no way of getting blood for a transfusion, so the doctor gave her an auto-transfusion by taking blood from her bleeding abdomen and pumping it back into her veins. She, too, lived.

June Salstrom and I were on our way to Swaziland to take some nurses to one of their homes. Of course we had to transport them in the pickup "ambulance." The back had a canopy over them. All was going well until we came to a "dip" in the dirt road. As soon as June saw the steepness of the dip, she applied the brakes, which gripped. I only remember seeing the solid wall of red clay. The truck rolled over, tossing us all out on the ground. I was knocked out for a short time. When I came to, I lifted my head, looked around, and said, "This is NOT heaven!" and promptly put my head back down on the dirt road in disappointment. I fully awoke shortly after. My first Zulu word was "*Siza!*" (help), which I repeatedly called out, while running down the road in the hope of someone could hear and help us. Finally, a man came along and he notified our hospital. No one was injured, but the hospital maintenance man had to come to tow us back to the hospital.

There are so many stories which could be told of God's wisdom, grace, provision, and mercy. So many could be told of patients who listened to the music and sermons played on the intercom into all the wards, as well as the morning prayers. Some responded to God's salvation through the death of Jesus Christ for forgiveness of sin to everyone who would repent and receive Him as their own Savior. Still, there were those who refused their opportunity, and went into a Christless eternity. That was always hard to realize.

Just because one goes to the mission field, it does not mean that one has learned all one needs to know about Christian living. I had to learn that it was better to know that something was done, than to be known as the doer of something.

Also, many times I had to pray that the Lord would keep me from the sin of sensitivity, yet sensitive to sin.

Language School

I had always wanted to speak Zulu, but one incident emphasized it more. It was early in my first five year term, so my vocabulary was rather limited. An old man with snake skins wrapped around his waist, was talking with me. I told him the best I could, and quoted Bible verses, how Jesus had died for his sins. It cut me to the core, when he took hold of the snake skins and strongly said. "**This** takes away my sin." One's heart sinks! This made me more determined to learn Zulu. Much later, June Salstrom led him to accept the Lord.

After five months, I was given mornings to learn Zulu from a S.A. minister, who spoke it like a Zulu, but the stress was more on the grammar. I still had to work in the afternoons, so it curtailed my learning. We also had a rule that, when on duty, the nurses could only speak English in order for them to be able to pass their government exams in English. This hampered practicing my Zulu.

Wayside Sunday Schools

Later I was given charge of the "Wayside" Sunday schools. "Wayside" means exactly that! During the week, I would teach the lesson to 16 nurses, who in turn would teach it to the children in the surrounding areas. On Sunday, the nurses would climb onto the pickup truck and would be driven along the dusty road, or path, to be dropped off by twos at the same designated place each week. As we got near the places, we would honk the horn. The children would drive the cattle nearby, which they were watching, and sit on the ground, or on the stones. They enjoyed singing choruses and listening to the Bible story via flannel graph material. Occasionally, they would have to jump up, run, and give a shrill whistle while waving a large stick over their heads, in order to control their cattle or goats, which were getting into a neighbor's cornfield. There were no fences!

We started another Sunday school about six miles down in the low veldt. I had purchased a 50-cc.motorized bicycle, and used it to go down the mountain road. Going down was great, but coming up was an entirely different story! The boulders and sand would let me go just a few yards before the motor would stop. It would stall when I tried to get the clutch out at the same time as I gave it gas. Just a few times I could get it to go, but only a little way, and it would stall again. The only other thing was to push it up the steep incline in the hot sun. My heart would pound, and perspiration was excessive. Not much later, I had to give up going to that Sunday school.

My sometimes trusty transportation

Once a year, we held a Sunday school rally on the hospital grounds. All the children would walk from their homes with their sleeping mat on their heads, a blanket on their back, and an enamel cup and a dish in their hands, to spend a weekend with us. They were housed in the small, old stone church, with its cold, cement floor and its rusty corrugated iron roof, as well as in other various buildings on the property. They lined up each mealtime to have their food dished up into their bowls. As they sat around on the grassy airplane runway, they would eat their food with their fingers. A few had a spoon. The etiquette for eating with their fingers was to dip into the porridge no further than the second knuckle. It was the technique of scooping it up into their mouths. They received three meals a day, which faithful women cooked for them in very large tripod black cast iron pots with fires burning underneath. After breakfast, they would gather in groups, scattered in various spots on the airstrip, for singing and listening to a Bible story. Then came lunch, and after lunch, there were different foot races and games, with the various Sunday schools competing against each other. Each group was eager to earn a prize. After supper, we had an evening service led by the hospital chaplain. The Zulus love to sing, so they also had singing contests between the eight different Sunday schools.

Ladies dishing up food

Etiquette of eating

On Sunday, after the regular church service and after lunch, they would put their blankets on their backs, their rolled-up grass mats on their heads, and with their cup and bowl in hand, the homeward journey would begin. Many even carried their younger brother or sister piggy-back. Some lived only a few miles away, but others lived eight to ten miles away. And they walked the stony paths barefoot. It was always hard to get them on their way, because they had had such a good time and had made new friends, or had seen friends from the year before. Yet, we knew that they had to reach home before dark. In Africa there is no twilight. When the sun goes down it is really dark within ten minutes.

Even as I write this my heart is overflowing with such joy in remembering those times.

Homeward bound

Relaxation along the Way

Since there was not much to do for entertainment or relaxation, no TV, radio, or car, Katie Gurzi and I decided to go for a hike on a bushy path along the mountain ridge. After about a half hour we found a spot on which to sit and look out over Swaziland. We were there about five minutes, when Katie spotted a snake on a rock nearby. Rather quickly we decided to end our excursion. On the way back to the hospital, as we approached the village store, we encountered some Africa men who had been drinking. Since it was already dark, we hurried even faster. We reached the mission safely, but were not allowed to be out alone again.

There were also occasions when I was so overtired that I would get depressed. Our enemy knows that, and attacks in ways one would not believe! I knew I was extremely exhausted, but I would always argue with myself, that God would give strength. One day, I was so down that I even doubted if God existed, but He immediately proved Himself to me as I experienced a very sharp pain in my right side, and I instantly cried out, "God, help me!" And I thought, how could I deny Him one second, and in the next second, cry out to Him for help if He didn't exist?? I learned that one's physical wellbeing has a lot to do with one's spiritual wellbeing.

Six months before I was due for my first furlough (now called home assignment) I was down in bed, with absolutely no strength left. After being in a horizontal position for a few days, I became very discouraged and began to cry, thinking that I had been a failure and would have to go home early. Just then, one of the missionaries came to tell me that another missionary, from another station had phoned and wanted to take me on an all-expense-paid two week vacation! Being so far away, there was no way that she could have known my condition. Yet she wanted me to go with her and another family to a cottage on the South Coast. I had no money to do such a thing, but I knew I needed help health-wise. We did go, and I enjoyed it to the extent that my tired body would allow itself to rejuvenate. After the two weeks, and as we were traveling back to the hospital, Christine said to me, "Bev, don't try to pay me back. Just do something for someone else." I have never forgotten that statement, but it does put one in debt all one's life. I try, to the best of my ability and resources, to do just that. What a lifelong challenge!!

The two-week vacation was like a band-aid for my condition. I got back to the States after my five and a half year term, but was just so utterly exhausted physically. Our mission required a physical, so I went to my doctor and he ordered a thyroid Basal Metabolism Rate test (BMR). It came back that I was minus 49, and minus 50 was the crisis point! So he immediately put me on a thyroid medication, which did the trick after a time. Later, I was able to complete my deputation schedule.

3

<u>Ending The First Phase</u>

<u>"Hiccups" on the Trek</u>

*B*efore my home assignment (furlough), I had asked the Field Council if I could come back three months earlier than the allotted 12 months, in order to have three extra months of Zulu language study. I also knew that I would have to return to Addington hospital in Durban for three months to retake and pass their exams in order to qualify as a Sister in their nursing requirements. I had failed two years earlier. It had been decided that I lacked three months of surgical nursing. How that was determined was hard to understand. I had a rather large file from my School of Nursing in the States, with detail proof of exactly how many patients, of what diagnosis, and the number of days I had been credited. Since they had no such record keeping, it seemed so unfair, but not to God. The Field Council gave me permission to return three months earlier, depending on meeting the Stateside Mission requirements.

South Africa's nursing system was much different. Changing a bandage required four forceps instead of two. The nurses were scheduled to go to lectures, but I could not go. When I would ask permission, I would be told that the ward had to be covered. End of conversation! So I would go back to rolling cotton balls, or making 4x4-inch gauze dressings to replenish their supplies, a pastime we all did when there was nothing else to do.

Also, their pronunciation of certain terms would not register with my brain. One time I was alone in the nurses' station when the phone rang. I bravely answered it, but I could not understand what type of patient they were sending. Finally, it came to me that they were sending an appendicitis patient. They would put the emphasis on a different syllable than I was familiar with hearing.

I had to take the oral and practical exam at the end of the three months. On the exam I made a couple of very small mistakes, and I knew I had. When I made those mistakes, the examiner just openly laughed at me, which made me more nervous. So I failed to be registered by the S. A. Nursing Association. They determined I had to do the three months all over. For me, this was a horrible hiccup.

Plans for the Return

After five and a half years, I left South Africa in June of 1961 to the challenge of my first furlough, now called home assignment. This is primarily to report to churches and individuals regarding events or situations and God's workings in those years. I also was very concerned about the recruitment of a pharmacist. I had been in charge of the pharmacy, along with my other duties, and I loved it, but it was just too much for me. So, in my meetings, I always announced the need of a pharmacist, but God didn't seem to influence anyone to volunteer.

I had been living with my parents during my home assignment, but things were not congenial. There were incidents that occurred when I thought of moving out, but since we all went to the same church, I thought it might reflect back on my parents, which I didn't want to happen. I was constantly being told that I would not be ready to go back to South Africa at the end of nine months. I just prayed to God that He would prove Himself to that person— and He did! Toward the end of the nine months, it became almost unbearable. I can remember not praying, but *telling* the Lord that no matter what would happen, I would not live at home when I returned on the next home assignment. Little did I realize what God had in mind.

My mother rode with me to Chicago, but that evening was not a pleasant one. We stayed at mission headquarters overnight, we then drove to a friend's house, who in turn took us out to O'Hare Airport, where I took off for my second term. About halfway out over the Atlantic Ocean, I had a "new experience." It was nothing dramatic, nor was it a release of things I had had to go through during those nine months at home. It was that God just seemed so much closer to me than ever before. I was silently basking in His grace, and enjoying every moment of it.

4

Back To Zululand

*T*he long trip over to South Africa was delightful. I was
met at the Jan Smuts Airport in Johannesburg by June
Salstrom, an R.N. from our mission hospital, and missionary
Ralph Christensen, from Jo'burg. As we were driving to
our Mission headquarters, June said, "Hey, Bev, did you
know that we have a new missionary?" I quickly asked, "Is
he a pharmacist?" She answered, "No. He's a general missionary." My heart sank, and I was so disappointed with the
Lord that he was not a pharmacist. But as I looked over at
Ralph driving, he had a grin from ear to ear, and you would
have to know Ralph to know the length of that grin!! It didn't
mean much to me at that instant, but as time passed, I came
to realize the meaning of it!

I stayed in Jo'burg a few days, until it was time to go to our TEAM annual conference in Pietermaritzburg. It was so wonderful to be back in South Africa with my real family in the Lord. No matter the hard or joyful times, the missionary's family is closer than any other. We cry together, pray together, bear each other's burdens, yes, and even disagree together. We are a close-knit family, and even now in our retirement.

New Missionary on the Trek

A day after my return to Jo'burg, I was in the kitchen of Marge and Dick Winchell, talking with their teenaged daughter, Marty. Marge came in with this new missionary and proceeded to introduce him to me. I have always been very shy around the opposite sex, so I barely greeted him, and rather abruptly turned around and proceeded to talk with Marty. I guess he got the message; shortly after that, he left the room.

A few days later, I was outside one of the missionary's home, waiting for June Salstrom to come out. I had begun to sense the missionaries "matching" Chuck and me together, and as I stood there, I sensed God saying, "Would you get married?" I can remember kicking a stone and saying rather disgustedly, "No, Lord, I came back to get the language." And that was that! Almost immediately, the Lord said, "Would you do it for My honor and glory?" The conversation ended there, with no further comment from me.

Toward the end of the week, the missionaries decided who was to ride with whom to the conference, since not everyone had transportation. They put me with two older single ladies in the same vehicle, which Chuck was to drive. It still didn't twig with me about their scheming. It all seemed like a natural arrangement, and it probably was the most feasible plan. We all chatted along the way, but Chuck said very little. I think I did most of the talking, just because I was so happy and excited to be back in South Africa. It was so wonderful to be winding our way down through the lush green hills, and even to stop for tea time at the Valley of a Thousand Hills. What pure joy!

From Pietermaritzburg, I took the bus down to the port city of Durban to retake the nursing course. I met with the Director of Nurses at the hospital to ask permission to begin the course, and was told that it would not start until the next week. So I asked permission to report back then. (The God of all time timed it for me.) So I immediately returned to 'Maritzburg by bus to attend the conference.

At the conference, when it was time for returning missionaries to give their testimonies, I repeated the end of Psalm 4:3b-4, "The Lord will hear when I call unto Him. Stand in awe and sin not." I stood in awe of what my Lord had done for me, and rejoiced in this fact. It was just so good to be back in South Africa. I didn't look forward to redoing my three months of surgical nursing in Durban, but I wanted to get it over before I went up to the mission hospital in Zululand. After a delightful week, I returned to Addington Hospital, reported in, received my uniform, my ward assignment, and my room allocation.

<u>Repeated "Hiccups"</u>

The first day on the ward, one of the doctors just said to no one in particular, "Nurse, what about this?" I happened to be the only one in the ward, had just come on duty, and was not acquainted with the patients. I could only say, "I don't know, doctor, I just came on duty." He turned around and looking straight at me and in a loud voice exclaimed, "Yankee!!" That really startled me, because I thought he would not be happy with my answer. But he continued by saying that he had been in Italy with American soldiers in WWII and held a great respect for Americans. God had worked on my behalf, and from then on this doctor sought me out and respected me.

Doctors who are specialists are referred to as "Sir." One day while going off duty with another nurse, we passed a doctor coming in, whom I recognized. I said "hello" to him, and the nurse reprimanded me rather strictly by saying, "Nurse Pfeiffer, you do not greet doctors, who are Sirs." Quite a difference in culture.

I had asked the head Sister if I could be excused with the other nurses in my group when they went for their classes. She said firmly that the ward had to be covered. Since the other nurses were mostly in the same group, that meant that I would have to stay behind. How could I learn their technique for changing bandages, catheterizations, and other things which are done so differently?

One day all the nurses left for their class, and I stood there rolling cotton balls. I said, "Lord, is this going to be the same thing all over again?" Just then, the Sister came to me and said, "Nurse Pfeiffer, the ward is covered. You may go to the class." I didn't wait for her to change her mind!

Another time as I was bathing a lady, I noticed a large lump on the left side of her abdomen. I reported it to the ward Sister, but nothing was done about it. A day later, as the doctor and the head Sister were examining the patient, they called me over and asked if I had seen it before, and why I had not reported it. I told them that I had told the ward Sister, who was also standing there. I don't know if anything developed because of the ward Sister not doing anything about it. But I surmised that it might have had something to do with the head Sister offering me the opportunity of becoming a ward Sister on her ward after I finished my three-month' course. A great offer, but my heart was anchored in the little Mosvold Mission Hospital at Ingwavuma, Zululand.

God's Intervention

Another intervention of God's was at the end of the three months, when I had to retake the oral and practical exams. This time, we were to have the most dreaded examiner. The nurses told horrible stories about her methods and how many she would fail. I was to be the first one to be examined. As I sat outside on the veranda waiting for them, I found myself reading a magazine, which I had not intentionally picked up.

I just felt so relaxed without realizing it. As the examiner and the co-examiner came around the corner, I saw that the co-examiner was the Sister from my ward. The government examiner held out her hand and we shook hands. The Sister on my ward had substituted for another Sister, because the originally chosen one was unable to be there that day. Later, I realized that I had made one very small mistake, and the Sister had gone to bat for me. When I returned to the dining room for lunch, I told the other nurses there that the examiner was not so bad. "She even shook hands with me!" **"Shook hands with you!!"** they all exclaimed almost in unison.

I was free to go back up country to my beloved Zululand ministry. A few months later, I received a letter stating that I had passed my exams and was now registered as a Sister under the Nurses' Association of South Africa, the equivalent of an R.N. in the States. What a time of rejoicing!!

Months later, I was in a store in Jo'burg and I saw one of the South African classmates who had been with me at Addington Hospital in Durban. She told me that another nurse, who had taken the three-month course, and myself, were the only ones out of the whole class that passed. It was wonderful to know how great was His working on my behalf for the exam, just by meeting this nurse so unexpectedly in a large store at the same counter!

During the three months in Durban, another missionary, Carolyn Tice, Chuck Smith, Louie and Marie, and I met at Carolyn's apartment for a weekly Bible study. That is where I began to know Chuck, and to realize I liked what I saw in him. Yet, I was so determined to be in the Lord's will, and conscious of Satan's desire to get me out of His will. I was constantly aware of wanting to do what God planned for me. I had seen other missionaries marry, and maybe one could not continue in missions either because of sickness — or one of them was not accepted by the Africans. So I watched Chuck very carefully.

God's Sense of Humor

It was also during this time that I really discovered the Lord's sense of humor. He has created us in His image — with a sense of humor, so He must have one also! It was a fun time between me and my Lord. Whenever I would test the Lord, I would tell Him that it didn't matter to me how things would turn out, I just wanted to have fun with Him!

And I really meant it! Here are some of the ways we had fun together — just my Lord and I.

Whenever I was off duty in Durban, I would go to church with Carolyn. As we sat in the balcony, I would ask the Lord to let Chuck come in right at 7:25 p.m. Many times it happened, and I would laugh inside. The times he didn't come at the right time, or not at all, I would always say to the Lord that I was satisfied with His will.

Another time, after I had gone up to Ingwavuma and Chuck was still studying Zulu in Durban, an older couple was getting married at another mission station about 70 miles away. I really wanted to go, but didn't want to go if Chuck would be there, because people might think that I went just because he would be there. The people with whom I was to ride to Magut kept asking me if I was going with them. I kept telling them I would let them know later. About the third time of them asking me, I wanted direction from the Lord. Just then the secretary of the hospital, Katie Gurzi, passed me on the path to the hospital. She said, "Hey, Bev, guess who I just talked to at the Durban book store — Chuck!" I just silently said, "Thank you, Lord!" and immediately told the Browns that I would ride with them to the wedding. I knew that Chuck could not get to Magut in time, since it was more than two-thirds of the distance from Durban. So I went to the wedding and enjoyed it.

Language School, Continued!

After my nurse's registration in Durban, I went to Ingwavuma for an extra three months of studying Zulu, and Chuck stayed in Durban to continue his Zulu studies with an older missionary. He had to wait for a government permit to come to Ingwavuma. I was studying on my own and took time to practice conversations with the laundry women as they folded the laundry out on the grass. I was diligent at first, but later thoughts of Chuck kept coming into my mind, crowding out my Zulu concentration. It bothered me, because I wanted to learn Zulu. So I decided to go to another mission station, Ndumu, 30 miles away in the low veldt. There a single nurse operated a clinic. It was quieter and had less going on, so I could fully devote myself to study. All was fine the first two days, but then my thoughts would often turn to Chuck. So I went to my Counselor in prayer. I remember saying that I WANTED to get the language, and I WANTED only His will. I reasoned with the Lord and said, "If Chuck and I were the only believers on an island, that still wouldn't mean he was the one for me." After deliberating with my Lord, I had real peace, and the rest of the week was good for studying.

After the Friday clinic, I went with the doctor, with patients on the back of the open five-ton truck, back up to the hospital. When I arrived, I thought I would just go into the hospital to see what things had happened while I was gone. I met Ruth Aronson, and the first thing that she said to me was, "Hey, Bev, did you hear that Chuck got his permit to come to Ingwavuma?" I was really disgusted and upset with my Lord, because I knew it would start all over. And it did!!

Within two weeks, Chuck arrived at Ingwavuma to get more oral practice in the language. He also worked part-time as a maintenance man, keeping the pick-up ambulance running, maintaining the diesel generator, etc. Then on the weekends, he visited a small church at the foot of the mountain. As time allowed during the week, he would visit with that pastor and help to thatch his hut. Since he was a radio operator in the Marines, he also maintained the radios between two isolated low-veldt mission stations and the hospital. He was the "ambulance" driver of either the pickup truck, or the five-ton lorry (truck). In other words, he was an all-around fellow — and an ordained minister.

5

Marriage On The Trek

African Customs

*I*n the African society, Christians get engaged in the church. The boy and his entourage sit on one side of the church, and the girl and her entourage sit on the other side. Then each of their entourage will stand up and testify for them separately. Following this, he will put the ring on her finger. There is no sign of emotions, such as kissing, or even holding hands.

God's Promise on the Trek

As I said before, thoughts of Chuck were almost con-stantly on my mind, yet I really wanted only the Lord's plan for my life. I watched him so closely, as to how he would fit in with the Zulus and with mission life. He treated all the single missionary ladies the same, which was easier for my timid personality. I was very happy and content being single. I always thought that marriage was a holy institution, but it was not for me, yet I knew I was being drawn to Chuck. There were times when Chuck would seem to warm up, and then it seemed like he would cool off. After some time, I told the Lord that I had to have an answer one way or the other. I could not go on with the spiritual see-saw. That evening I thought I would get the answer in my prayer time, but it came in a different way.

I had been reading through the Psalms by taking the date of the month for the first Psalm, then adding 30 to it each time, and thus reading five Psalms at a time each day. Thus, I read through all the Psalms in a month. I had been doing this, and so I continued. It was May 23, 1963, that I read Psalm 113 and verse 9, which says "He maketh the barren woman to keep house, and to be the joyful mother of children. Praise ye the Lord." (KJV) The words "barren" and "joyful mother of children" jumped out at me. I had been told that I probably never would be able to have children, due to a hormonal deficiency, yet God gave me that verse. I knew that to be a mother I would have to be married, so I took God at His word, and made it His promise to me. I had His assurance and my spiritual see-saw slowed down. The fulfillment didn't come until a year later, and the Lord tested me during that year, whether I could still hold Him to the promise by faith.

We nurses were so understaffed that we asked help from another mission hospital. They loaned us one for three months, and as she was coming, I wondered if Chuck might like her. I just had to trust the Lord for His will, and I told God that if Chuck was not the one for me, that I would be satisfied with His will. The other nurse came, and my trepidation was dispelled as she was much older.

The Promise Fulfilled

Dr. and Gerry Morrill started to have a game night on Fridays, when any of the missionaries could go to their house for relaxation. Many of us would go, and it really helped me to observe Chuck even more. But since he had never paid extra attention to me, I would often say to my Lord, "Lord, I know you have promised, but WHEN?" Finally, one night, Chuck asked me to marry him, and I said, "Yes." His next question was, "Do you want to pray about it?" My reply was, "No, I have prayed about it."

It wasn't long before he had everything planned. Previously, I had committed myself to be a counselor at a camp in Jo'burg with some other missionaries. That entailed my going to Durban by train, and then another train to Jo'burg. Chuck thought of some reason that he had to go to Durban that same weekend by car. Another thing was that we had to have permission from our Field Council to marry, which depended upon our being on the field for at least two years and having completed language study, which we both had done. They were meeting the week before we went to Durban, and Chuck asked them to keep it secret until we were engaged. We wanted the Zulus and the missionaries to hear it at the same time. They gave us their permission and blessing before the engagement. We both went separately to Durban.

In African society, a boyfriend and girlfriend are never together alone. They always have a go-between who communicates messages to those involved. In order to keep our testimonies clear and upright, before both God and man, we were very careful. However, we wanted our engagement to be more private.

So how do two in love carry on a courtship under those conditions?? Well, necessity is the mother of invention. Our station had an inter-house telephone system whereby every person, or house, had a specific number of rings, created by turning the handle of the phone. For instance, one doctor had a long ring, another doctor had a long and short ring, another house had three short rings, etc. Of course, everyone in the houses heard whose ring was sounding. There was a station rule that there should not be any ringing after 9:00 p.m. So Chuck and I would pick up the phone, without ringing anyone, at a pre-determined time and cautiously ask, "Is that you?" In the midst of our conversation, if we heard a click as when someone would pick up the receiver, we would quickly put ours down, without even saying "goodbye." Thus we carried on our courtship.

In order to go to Jo'burg for the camp, I had to go to Gollela, the last train stop at the bottom of the mountain on the border with Swaziland. One of my housemates, along with the wife of one of our doctors, offered to take me down the winding narrow mountain road on Thursday morning. Before we left, Shirley Preece prayed, "Lord, help Bev to get everything done in Durban that she has to do before going to Jo'burg." I was bursting inside, and amusedly thought, "You don't know the half of it!!"

It took 23½ hours to travel the 250 miles, including 99 stops. The train would just pick up steam when we would start slowing down for a stop, which usually meant picking up a farmer's milk cans. Time didn't bother me, because I was just basking in the Lord's plans for me. I knew I loved Chuck very much, and that I had tested the Lord for His perfect will. Now, He was showing me beyond a shadow of doubt that what He had promised, He was now bringing it to pass.

I arrived in Durban on Friday and went directly to Concord Missionary Home. This is a place established specifically for missionaries stationed up-country to come for rest, or for buying supplies in Durban. Chuck drove his VW Beetle to Durban and arrived in the late afternoon. He had eaten sour porridge at an African meeting, and for some reason he got very sick with a terrible headache, temp, and vomiting. He went to his room, and a good long sleep helped.

Engagement

On Saturday evening, he took me out for dinner, and afterwards we went to one of our missionary's home in Durban North. Chuck had pre-arranged with Irl McCallister to take his family out of the house, so that it could use it for a half-hour for Chuck to propose and for us to pray together. We wanted our engagement to be more private. However, we did leave a typed message for our station head to be read to the missionaries at 8:00 p.m., back at the hospital. This is the time we designated for our private engagement in Durban. Also, the same message was to be read in Zulu the next morning at 7:00 a.m., after morning chapel.

As we approached the stairs leading to the front door of the house, we heard voices speaking what we recognized as Zulu. I turned to Chuck and said, "Oh, Irl has put on some Zulu tapes!" A few steps further, I recognized that it was a conversational tone. As we reached the door, someone opened it and there stood Beauty, their house maid, talking on the telephone! We were a little surprised, because remember that a boyfriend and girlfriend were never seen together alone, and here we stood!! Beauty just kept on talking on the phone, so Chuck asked her in Zulu where was the "Umfundisi" (preacher). She replied, "In town," and just kept on talking. Chuck had made arrangements with the McCallisters for the use of their home from 7:30 to 8:00 p.m., and the time was running out! So he asked Beauty if he could use the phone, and she finally hung up. While he pretended to call someone, Beauty came over to where I was sitting and started to entertain me. So Chuck told her it was OK. and that she could leave, which she did.

Chuck proceeded to propose, when we heard Beauty in the kitchen. She had been taught to make tea for company, and as we heard the rattling of dishes, we knew what she was doing. So, once again, Chuck told her that everything was OK and she could go. Finally, we were alone, and Chuck proposed, placed the ring on my finger, and had just finished praying, when the telephone rang. Chuck answered it. It was Dick Winchell, who also was stationed in Durban. He was surprised to hear Chuck's voice, and asked who was there. Chuck said, "We are. . .uh, Beauty and I." As soon as they hung up, the McCallisters, with their five children, came bursting through the door. The kids then realized why they had to go for a walk on the beach that night, when they really didn't want to do it. Flo McCallister had baked a cake that day, so we all went over to the Winchell's for a celebration.

Dick opened the door and was so surprised to see Chuck and me in the group. Then everything dawned upon him! Irl was on the Field Council, and had known about the plan, but Dick was not on the F.C. Dick, who later became Director of TEAM, was so witty that he kept us in stitches for over an hour. He was the one who first changed our names from Chuck and Bev to "Chev and Buck." Who can ever say that God does not have a sense of humor! And we enjoy His creative attributes.

Mr. and Mrs. Henry Pfeiffer
request the honour of your presence
at the marriage of their daughter

Beverly Jean
to
Rev. Charles L. Smith

on Saturday, the thirtieth of May
nineteen hundred and sixty-four
at 2 o'clock p.m.
Mosvold Mission Hospital Chapel
Ingwavuma, Zululand

Reception
to follow

Wedding announcement

Back at the hospital, Dr. Morrill called a station meeting, and without anyone knowing it, he put a tape recorder behind their drapes. He read the announcement, and all was quiet for about 20 seconds. Then all the missionaries began to speak at once. Some of the comments were priceless; others were figments of people's imaginations. But everyone seemed happy for us.

The next morning in chapel, the same announcement was made. Dr. Morrill again read it in Zulu, and again recorded the reaction. There was silence for about 20 seconds, then the sound of shuffling feet, and the murmuring of Zulu as the thought sank into their minds.

I left Durban the next day on the train for the camp in Jo'burg. The train stopped in Pietermaritzburg for about ten minutes, and to my surprise June Salstrom and Mary Morrill came to the train to greet me. They were both in nurses' training for Midwifery and for R.N. They gave me a beautiful blue vase, which I still have as a reminder of their good wishes. I can still see them running alongside of the train as we pulled out of the station. What joy to see them share in my joy! When I reached Jo'burg, all the missionaries were just as happy for me. God proved Himself true to His promise to me in Psalm 113:9. The second part of the promise was to come later.

A week later, I returned to the hospital via the long train ride. Instead of hearing the "click, click, click" of the train, I kept hearing "Chuck, Chuck, Chuck"!

When I returned to the hospital, the reception from both the missionaries and the Africans was overwhelming. It was reflected in their eyes and smiles. Since we were older, and had met the field's requirements, we set our wedding date for May 30, 1964.

During those six weeks, Chuck could walk me home from the hospital in the daytime, but never at night. At our noon break, he would come to my house, and we would plan as much as we were able. We both wanted a flawless testimony before our colleagues and our African friends. So if Chuck came at noon time, and no one else was to be in the house, we would take our chairs outside in full view. Facing each other, we would continue our courtship. Some would think that it was a hindrance, but we just thought of it as a game.

Precious Lessons

God was teaching me so much about Himself, and I was basking in His love for me. One of the most memorable lessons happened one day as I was walking to the hospital, I thought, "God, how can Chuck love me?" The immediate response was, "How can I (God) love you?" I didn't understand God's love for me, yet I would not give it up. And so with Chuck, I didn't understand his love for me, yet I was not willing to give him up. I marveled at his choice of me, when there were several other single girls who were pretty and gifted. I was neither. Still, I could say that out of a world of so many people, how did God allow me to become one of His? There were times when I had to say to the Lord, "Stop! I cannot hold any more blessings."

Some may think that we were really restricted in our courtship. We just considered it fun, and we still enjoy the memories. Our first time of being alone together was when we went on our honeymoon to a self-contained flat (apartment) at Amanzintoti (Sweetwaters), on the South Coast just below Durban.

We had just six weeks to plan the wedding from the distance of 250 miles from Durban. Actually, I didn't plan it, but God brought people into the situation that, in a most Christ-like way, did most of the planning yet gave me the impression that I was planning it myself! Marie Padmore suggested that her aunt make my dress, which entailed my going to Durban three times. Flo McCallister guided me into choosing the pattern and material for the dress. Gerry Morrill set up the schedule for a meal for those who were planning to come. Betty Taylor planned the reception in their yard. The European (white) ladies in the village gave me a lovely bridal shower. The magistrate sent over extra benches from the courthouse to add to the ones we had in the newly built chapel. Village ladies sent flowers and plants for decorating the church. All of it was so lovely.

6

<u>Trekking Together</u>

<u>The Wedding</u>

The wedding party

The big day!

*O*n the day of the wedding, May 30, 1964, T.E.A.M. missionaries from most of South Africa arrived early to have lunch. Gerry Morrill organized the meal and sent a large plate of food to my house for me before the ceremony.

That morning I looked out my window and saw people bringing wedding gifts to me. For a slight moment I got "cold feet" and wanted to run away. But that thought was quickly dashed! It was a perfect day in every respect. The church was decorated with frangipani, a white petal flower with a pink center, and some red hot pokers — a brush-like group of small round very red clusters on the end of long stems. Most of the floral decorations were created by the European ladies from the local village. Dr. Taylor acted for my father and walked me down the aisle. I had three bridesmaids — Wilma Gardziella, Claire Christopherson, and Caroline Tice — dressed in three shades of blue. We all carried artificial floral bouquets. Chuck also had three groomsmen, Dr. Morrill, Dr. Maxwell, and Dr. Cook. The folding pump organ was played by Jon, the teenaged son of Dr. Morrill; Harry Lloyd sang; and Rev. David Greene performed the ceremony.

Someone wrote this insightful verse; which I have often recited:

He knows, He loves, He cares.
Nothing this thought can dim,
He gives the very best to those,
Who leave the choice with Him.

After the reception, we changed and rode away down the dusty, potholed, winding road in our VW. We had to get through passport control between Swaziland and South Africa at the Gollela gate before it closed. The red clay dust left on the car revealed the Vaseline message "Just Married" on the windows. Also, someone had put stones in the hubcaps to make noise as we traveled. We just made it through the gate with ten minutes to spare. Our first night was spent at the Ghost Mountain Inn at Mkuzi. This was so named because the legend has it that the Zulu chief, Shaka, would throw his enemies down the high, steep, sheer cliffs to their deaths. It was not hard to imagine.

After the Honeymoon

The next morning, we traveled on down to a self-contained flat at Amanzintoti on the South Coast, just below Durban. We had a lovely two weeks, with our flat being right on the Indian Ocean. However, May in the Southern Hemisphere is wintertime, and the beach is not as appealing as in the summer time.

When we returned to Ingwavuma, I took up residence with Chuck in the house he had occupied while the Snavelys and their five children were on furlough. Being so conscious of boy-girl relationships, that evening as I was brushing my teeth, I thought, "What am I doing here in *his* house?" And for a split second, I wanted to run out and go to the Amas' house, where I had lived. Because housing was usually a factor, it was easier for us single girls to change housing to accommodate families going and coming on furlough. In my first five years, I moved six times.

Sing Sing

About four months later, we heard that the Snavelys were coming back in two months and would need the house. The only other place to go was to "Sing Sing." This was at one time a single-car garage, and later, another half was added to it. Two nurses had lived in it previously. It had two bedrooms, a living room, and a small added-on room for a kitchen. The name came about because there was an outside door to each room. This allowed a nurse to be called out at night without disturbing anyone. The kitchen had a sink with a drain emptying into a bucket underneath on planks to catch the water. There were no cupboards or counters. However, Chuck planned a new layout, traveled to Vryheid, 150 miles away, bought the lumber and counter top material, and drove back with all this inside and on top of our VW Beetle. It was to be an L-shaped counter, which he built as a single unit. When he tried to put it into the house, he had forgotten that the angle was larger than the door way. So it meant he had to cut it and piece it together again after he got it in the house.

I am one who enjoys challenges. It is a good thing, because on the mission field, there are enough to make life interesting.

Chuck had come home one afternoon and said that the Ingwavuma river, at the foot of the mountain, was very high and a truck was lying on its side in the middle. He related that if an ambulance call came from the other side of the river, he could not cross it. As usual, the impossible become possible in God's plan.

Sure enough, that night, an ambulance call came in from across the river. He had to go! Chuck loaded the back of the pickup truck with bags of cement and the informer to weigh it down. I sat in the front; at the time I was about six-plus months pregnant. As we approached the river, the informer got out and walked across the river in the beam of the headlights to gauge the depth of the water. Just as we started up out of the river, the engine stalled. Praise the Lord, it restarted right away. God got us across and enabled us to bring the person to the hospital.

Full-Time Church Ministry

We had the enjoyment of our little Sing Sing for six months, when we heard that they needed it for another South African couple who was coming to take over maintenance from Chuck. The Field Council wanted Chuck to be in full-time church work, which would necessitate moving to another station. The station that was suggested was Magut, 75 miles away. It had been vacant for quite some time, and the weeds were waist-high. We traveled there, went inside to measure for some window curtains, and saw several wide cracks from the ceiling to the floor. Chuck had just finished making over Sing Sing, and I thought he had even a larger job on hand. In the midst of all of this, we heard a knock on the front door. When we opened it, there stood a salesman who wanted to know if we wanted to buy a portable Singer sewing machine. After he left, we burst out laughing at God's sense of humor. The driveway into the property led to the kitchen door, and EVERYONE used it. This man parked there, but walked through all the weeds to the front door. The F.C. decided not to send us to Magut.

There was one other option. That was to go to Mangwazane, a station that used to house a school for Africans. But the government took over the schools, so it was a station with many empty stone buildings inhabited by all kinds of snakes. We called it "Snake Park." However, this station was occupied by another couple, who were leaving the Mission yet taking their time to do so.

The only other opening was to go 30 miles further into the low-veldt to live with a single, older nurse, who ran a clinic. That would be great, but I was about seven months pregnant, and would probably have to have a caesarean section. I would have to travel to Pietermaritzburg, 250 miles away, plus the 30 miles from Ndumu. Ndumu would add another hour to get through the sandy road conditions. Due to my hormonal problem, I didn't know my due date, which added to the stress. So we packed our belongings into our 45-gallon drums and stored them at the hospital. The people arrived and began to move their belongings into the house. I had just a couple boxes left that I moved outside. It was then that I realized the reality of not having a home to call our own, as well as having to travel the long distance for a probable caesarean section. A lot of thoughts passed through my mind; what if the baby wanted to come on our way down to the city? Chuck was not a medical person. There were no large hospitals on the way. (When S.A. was settled, the towns were spaced about 30 miles apart, the distance that they could travel by oxen and covered wagons in a day.) So many thoughts raced through my mind, but just then Chuck came and said we were going on down to Ndumu. We then packed the car and made our way to Ndumu, where Eleanore Erikson greeted us with her usual warm self.

Don's Birth on the Trek

We were to stay with Eleanore until my appointment with the doctor in "'Maritzburg" about six weeks later. Yet, the God of all time timed it perfectly. The F.C. wanted us to come to Vryheid, which was our field headquarters, for Chuck to meet with the Field Council. This was over 100 miles away, with partly all sandy or rough roads. We did the trip, and stayed there for a week, until the date of the doctor's appointment. The road from Vryheid to 'Maritzburg was all paved, but a longer distance. We arrived with little time to spare, and as I was hurrying, I began to feel slight cramps. I told the doctor as he examined me, and he thought they were false labor pains, but he wanted me nearby for two weeks. We had already made arrangements for me to stay with some other single missionaries at Union Bible Institute up the mountain. That evening my pains grew stronger, and other symptoms occurred, so we had to go quickly to the hospital. Before when we arrived at 'Maritzburg, we had checked at the hospital to enquire if I did go into labor, should I stop there and check in first, or go directly to the Obstetrics ward. The clerk told me that we should check in first. So when we got there in the wee hours of the morning, Jeanette Eckel and I sat on the bench, waiting our turn after four other people. Finally, we got to the desk and I told him my name and for OB. He hardly looked at me, and said, with a wave of his hand, "OB!! Don't stand there! Get on up!!"

So while Chuck was parking the car, Jeanette and I made our way around the corner, doubled up with laughter, and waited for the lift (elevator). One of our nurses from Mosvold was at the same hospital, taking a midwifery course. As I was being walked down the corridor, we saw each other and momentarily stopped to greet. However, the nurse with me said, "Jane, this is an emergency." So we hurried on to the room, even though I didn't feel it was such a great hurry. I got on the examining table, and the nurse said, "You're having a contraction, aren't you?" I said, "No." Then she had me feel my abdomen, and I realized the extent of it. The only medication I needed was a small dose of Valium. When the doctor got there, he said, "Get her into surgery, STAT!" So I entered the surgical room, went to sleep, and woke up in a room with the news that we had a beautiful baby boy, whom we named Donald Lee Smith. Many missionaries wondered at our predicament of having to travel so far to the hospital, but I thought of Mary riding on a donkey, with a gift far more precious than even my joyful gift. God taught me about His trust through it all.

In the meantime, when Chuck was with me in the labor room, they said the doctor would come in at 9:00 a.m. So about 6:00, Chuck decided to go back up to UBI to shave and clean up. He had just arrived there when they greeted him at the door and said he had a son. So he then came back down to me, and also made arrangements to stay at the YMCA in town, since he could not stay with the Amas.

I had very good care at Grey's Hospital, and each day I felt much stronger. After ten days, the doctor said we could go home. It was good news, but where was "**home**"? Since the family had not yet vacated the station at Mangwazane, where we were to go, the field council decided we could go to the Children's Home at Vryheid and stay in the guest house on the same property. The Children's Home was a very large house where all the children from families up-country stayed, under the capable supervision of two single ladies. They provided all the home care while away from their parents. So we drove the 150 miles to our next accommodations.

We had one room with a very small electric heater, a hot plate, a few dishes, a bed with bedding, and a separate bathroom. June is in the middle of winter, and Vryheid, at a higher altitude, could get very cold. We even had a little snow. The Guest House was made of cement blocks with a cement floor. We had come from the warmer part of South

Africa with just our suitcases, and we were FREEZING!! Donnie would actually turn blue when I bathed him.

Chuck is not one to just sit around, and the situation got to him. So after about a week, he asked the F.C. if we could go back to the hospital and stay in Dr. Bennett's house, since they had gone on furlough, to which they acquiesced. We didn't wait around for them to change their minds, but loaded up our VW and started on the trip back to Mosvold Mission Hospital.

Bennetts' house was a family-size house with very little furniture. It had a two-seated settee, two chairs, a dining room table, and a bed. The kitchen had a full-size stove and a refrigerator. We were able to get into our drums, in which we had stored our belongings, in order to get out some kitchen essentials, clothes, bedding, and such. We both were more satisfied, because Chuck could go up to the garage and help with various projects. Even though the house was also made of cement blocks, the climate was warmer. Surprisingly, even in the midst of all this, Donnie thrived.

So we were patiently waiting for the other missionaries to vacate the station at Mangwazane in the Ubombo district. Finally, the news came that we could move over there. Chuck borrowed the hospital's five-ton Bedford lorry (flatbed truck) and loaded our belongings on it. He had to make a trip over with the stove and refrigerator, and to make sure the generator would start. The next day, I took Dr. Morrill's Helflinger (similar to an open Land Rover) with Donnie in the bed part of his pram sitting directly on the front floor of the vehicle. The distance was about 30 miles of dust, potholed, with half-hidden boulders. Every time I bounced over them the undercarriage would scrape and little Donnie's eyes would get so big! It meant going down the mountain, through the low veldt, and climbing back up another rocky mountain road with its twists and turns.

7

<u>Our Next Home On The Trek</u>

*A*fter the two-hour excursion, we made it! I remember getting Donnie into the house, sitting down with him in a dimly lighted room (no electricity). Even with the stove, refrigerator, and everything piled up in the center of the room, I said to myself after six weeks of living like vagabonds with a new baby, *"We're home*!!" What joy filled my heart in the midst of such turmoil. Chuck followed with another load of smaller articles packed in the VW, and arrived about 45 minutes later. He soon erected our bed and cleared a path so we could move around. We just used our Coleman lantern for a few nights, until we could get the generator running properly.

We had a good night's sleep, and awoke the next morning with the enthusiasm of new- home occupants to settle in with our own room arrangements, etc. Having been married just over a year, we didn't take long to unpack and get that "settled-in" feeling. Donnie was good and slept a lot in his pram, which helped.

Mangwazane Mission Station had been a boarding school for African children before the government took it over and closed it several years earlier. So the long rough, dirt driveway was lined with many empty rough stone buildings. The house we lived in was at the end of the driveway. This was a seven-room, rough stone building erected by a former Norwegian missionary with foot-thick walls. There were no halls, so each room led into another. It had a veranda (porch) on the back entrance with two doors. One led into the first room and the second one led into the middle room. The third room had a door leading to the outside. The right side of the house had three rooms also, but only the middle one had an outside door which opened up to its own rather large veranda. Off this was another long and narrow room which Chuck used as an office. This also had an outside door to the front veranda. All the doorways had crudely made screen doors.

The middle room on the left side of the house became our kitchen. As you entered the room, there was a single-drain sink in the corner. Under the sink there were flat wooden planks with a bucket under the drain. That left very little space to stack dirty dishes. A piece of oil cloth surrounded the area to hide the contents. There were no cupboards or work space. So once again, Chuck started to map out another kitchen for the first room, which had a nice large window. However, upon examination, he found the flooring to be only a very thin layer of cement over black dirt. So before any more renovations, he had to dig out the extra dirt to pour in substantial cement to make it suitable for tile squares. After this was done, he again went the long distance to Vryheid to buy materials and load them all on, and in, the VW Beetle. He took everything up to the hospital, where they had the saw and tools to cut out the kitchen cupboards. When that was done, he transported all the pieces back to Mangwazana and reassembled them there. It was so wonderful to have a double sink, lots of cupboards, plenty of counter work space, and a tile floor.

Since both Chuck and I had come out as single missionaries, there were certain things we had duplicates of, such as tableware, dishes, linens, etc. We had to cook on a gas stove by using two propane tanks—one as a switch over. We would tease each other about using "his" or "her" items. After we'd finally settled, Chuck started out to survey the area and to make contact with some church leaders.

Renovation

Our water supply was rain water collected from the house's corrugated iron roof. The rain ran down the drain pipes into the containers. One side of the house filled the large cement underground tank, while the other side filled three 500-gallon connecting galvanized iron tanks situated upon larger cement slabs. When the first tank filled up, it overflowed into the next connecting tank, and so on. They all had a screen on the top to prevent leaves and other things from getting into them. We used this water for drinking and cooking. The underground tank held water for other purposes. We obtained this water by pumping it out with the established hand pump. Not having running water in the house bothered Chuck. He believes that martyrs are born; not made. So he put a 45-gallon drum up on the roof and connected plastic tubing for the water to enter the house by gravity. This had to be pumped up from the underground tank.

Julia with Donnie

Donnie pumping water

We had a bucket system, so he wanted to make a septic system. He first started digging in one softer area, but as he got down about 3 feet, he saw a snake come out of the side of the hole. We went down the path to contact the pastor, who came up. As the men were poking around in the hole, they counted **seven different** kinds of snakes coming out of the sides. Needless to say, Chuck abandoned that spot.

He also wanted to cut the grass with a push lawn mower, so he proceeded to clear the area of stones. He soon found several wriggling baby snakes under almost every stone. After that, a machete worked just fine to cut grass.

The next spring, before the rains, Chuck decided to clean the water tanks. He started with the underground one, emptied it out, and found that it was relatively clean. He proceeded to the upright tanks, and found dead lizards, spiders, and even small snakes in them. This was our drinking water!

8

Life At "Snake Park"

*T*he following incidents are not told to conjure up sensationalism, or to think that we were brave. They are related as truth, only to show God's constant watch-care and protection through the two years (1965-1967) we lived at "Snake Park" — Mangwazane.

The Africans have a keen sense, and an eye, for snakes. The birds also make a different noise if one is near them. One time the birds were making a real commotion, and Pastor Magagula and his wife, Vinah, were nearby the large eucalyptus tree outside our kitchen. Magagula threw a large stick (a knob kerrie) high up in the tree. The snake fell down onto a lower branch. They kept asking me, "Do you see it?" I kept saying, "No!", until the sun happened to shine on its belly, illuminating it. Magagula kept throwing the stick up and finally knocked it to the ground, which dazed it. He struck it twice, but the snake revived and slithered away. Magagula said that snake would always be mean, because it had been wounded.

Chuck was gone for the day. Donnie was in his playpen in the living room, and I was doing things around the house. Once, as I entered the living room, I happened to catch sight of something on the screen of the screen door. It was fairly long, slightly bent and was *green!* I immediately grabbed Donnie and ran out of the kitchen door, down the path to the house of our young pastor. I told them what I had seen and asked for their help. It was then that I realized I had done a foolish thing. I didn't know if the snake was on the inside or the outside of the screen, and we would have to sleep there that night. The pastor and his wife came up. Vinah went through the inside of the house, and Magagula went on the outside, and around the building. He found the snake and killed it.

We were alone on the station and had nothing much to fill our hours, except to prepare Bible studies and to enjoy our son. So every Sunday, for a few months, we took Donnie outside to take his picture. One Sunday afternoon, Chuck had him in his arms close to his shoulder. I went just in front of him to open the screen door. As I pushed it open, and swung around to the left, while still holding the door, I looked down and saw a snake already spitting at Chuck's heel. I just said "Snake!!", and Chuck took off! The snake just turned around and went to the other side of the house. *A definite answer to prayer.* There was a cement sidewalk and porch on that side of the house, and the snakes seemed to like to bask in the warm sun on the nice warm cement. We never went outside without keeping our eyes down and looking out for slithering snakes. It was so automatic, that I continued to do it for many years later, even while on furlough.

We also had to contend with black scorpions hiding in the dark corners of our kitchen cupboards. Geckos scampered around freely, mostly on the walls and ceiling, but they never fell on us.

9

Joyful Surprises At Mangwazane

Our famous driveway

The "driveway" (if you can call it that) from the dirt road up to the top of the mountain ran through a farmer's field. Driving it necessitated stopping your vehicle, getting out, opening a gate, getting back into the car, driving it through, and getting out to close the gate. Then, a little further on, a repeat of the same. It also included bumping over cattle crossings, which consisted of round iron pipes spaced evenly over a large hole underneath. This path was about a quarter mile of washed-out gullies, rocks, and half-submerged boulders, with tall grass right up to the sides. At the end, by the old empty schoolhouse, it made a horseshoe turn and continued up the hill for another 300 yards to our house. We never could hear any vehicle coming. The only way we knew if we had company was when we would be in the kitchen and see a car in the driveway, or if someone knocked on the door. So we had some good surprises.

One such time was when Dick Winchell, his family from Durban, and four overseas visitors had told us that they would like to come for tea on their way over to the hospital. So I baked several things, and had it all set out for them, since they said they would be in a hurry to get over to Ingwavuma. Usually, tea time is between 3 and 4 p.m. When it came to be 5 p.m. and they were a no-show, I thought that they just went on to Ingwavuma. We had no phone or any way that they could contact us, so I put everything away. Just a half-hour later, I looked out the kitchen window to see nine adult people untangling themselves to get out of this small station wagon, and they were not small! I ran out to meet them and almost immediately said, "Can you stay for supper?" All of a sudden, I thought, "What do I have?" As they looked around the station, I began the meal. I used all the rice I had, and carefully measured the water trying to increase the quantity. We had been to Jo'burg the week before and had some hot dogs, which were a luxury for us. So I counted them, and there were just enough for each person to have one. I also opened two tins of vegetables. So we ate our meager supper, but everyone seemed satisfied. And the teatime items served as dessert. God increased the "jar of oil" just as He had for the widow woman in the Old Testament.

Sunday afternoon was always very quiet and sometimes lonely. We had no phone or T.V., and the small portable radio only provided limited evening transmission. But every so often we would hear a plane just above the trees. We would run out to a clearing in the yard, just in time to see Harold Stevens' tiny plane circle around, tip its wings and hear his voice over his p.a. system saying, "Hi, Chuck and Bev! I'm just on my way over to the hospital." And off he would go, leaving us with a warm joyful feeling.

We also had some mulberry trees on the property, and being one that cannot see things go to waste, I picked a large amount and baked about six pies. I followed with a large tuna casserole. Just as I was taking the casserole out of the oven, Dr. and Mrs. Cook and their three sons drove up. Ruth said, "Bev, can we just have some water for the boys?" Having driven up from Durban on their way to Ingwavuma, they ran out of water and diverted to us. I immediately satisfied them and cajoled them to stay for supper. After seeing I had plenty, and it was all ready, they agreed. Especially when young Steven saw all the pies and exclaimed, "Boy, Auntie Bev can sure bake a lot!" Again and again, God proved Himself faithful as our Provider.

Ministry at Mangwazane

After our initial renovations, we settled in well to the ministry to which we were assigned.

Being a station with several empty school buildings, it became a place for the area African churches to have their official quarterly meetings. Africans like big meetings, not just for the business, but also for fellowship. The women came with their paraphernalia — a large grass-woven sleeping mat, enamel dishes, enamel cup, a blanket — all neatly balanced on their head, and often with a small child strapped to their back. This was a normal sight. (I have often seen a woman walking along a path with a heavy portable wooden Singer sewing machine on her head, a small child strapped to her back, and knitting as she walked along. (They begin to teach their very small children the sense of head balance by placing a cup of water on their heads. It is not only for the sense of balance, but it also helps to develop and strengthen the neck muscles.)

The women of the Mangwazane church did all the cooking in 30- to 35-gallon black cast iron pots. We would have the most delicious white rice with slightly curried onions, cut-up pieces of beef with some tomatoes. This all cooked for a few hours over a small fire under the big pots. Sometimes the game reserve warden would cull out over-populated gazelles, and the men could get the meat free. It would be butchered and hung from a tree — with flies covering most of it.

The meetings would begin at 7:00 a.m., break for tea and a slice of bread, resume until 1:00 p.m., break for free time until

4:00 p.m., and supper. Then the evening meeting from 7:00 p.m. until they were finished around 10:00 p.m. The business meetings were in the daytime, and the Bible teaching was in the evening. The Zulus love to sing, have perfect pitch, and need no instruments. No meeting is without 30 to 45 minutes of singing in the beginning. It consists of the congregation, solos, quartets, small groups, etc. To announce a presentation, one would walk to the emcee and give a paper of intention with their title, like "song birds," "Omama (mothers)," etc. If children did poorly, the people would applaud all the louder. Never were they embarrassed. The people would sit all day for three days on backless wooden benches crowded together with no space between them. The intense heat was aggravated by the galvanized-iron roof, ceiling-less small church — which enhanced, the odor of bats to a high degree. **They did this to worship God!!**

Chuck would preach the Sunday service to the few members who lived nearby. Being near the top of the mountain with a small population, large ravines and all bush area made it difficult for the people to come to church. Therefore, Chuck would visit some of the outlying district churches and pastors. He also carried Bibles and Zulu study books in his VW. People knew this and often would stop him to buy some literature.

Another Trek Member!

We expected our second child in 1966. This time we had to travel down the dirty, dusty mountain road to go the long distance again to Pietermaritzburg. We were aware of the trip, but Chuck came home late one night and said that the car's clutch cable had broken. It had to be fixed in case I began labor. So he took a lantern and proceeded to fix the cable in the dark driveway.

A few days later, we made the trip with Donnie for another child's birth. There was no place for Chuck and Donnie to stay in Pietermaritzburg, so they traveled back to Mangwazane. Kenny was born the next day, but Chuck only found out two days later. A telegram was sent to Ubombo, but the post office closes on the weekend. He waited until we would be discharged ten days later before he came for us. Then he saw Kenny for the first time.

Donnie was fascinated with his little brother. Kenny had some instances when he would cry for long periods of time. Years later, we found out that he had allergy problems, causing internal pain. He never broke out with a rash, but had these terrible stomach pains. He was tested, and we found out that tomatoes, gasoline, cigarette smoke, and several other items — even sunshine — troubled him. None of these bother him now.

During the time I was gone, Julia, our house help, baked Chuck pumpkin pie, cinnamon yeast rolls, cake, and coffee cake and fed him well. She had had very little schooling and could not read English, but she learned well from being taught. Also, I came home to a spotless house. She was a rare gem!

Little Boys — and Church

As a family, we often went with Chuck to visit other churches. One time I was sitting in the back row with Kenny in my arms, and Julia was caring for Donnie. During the kneeling prayer time, Chuck felt a little tug on his jacket. Looking around, he saw Donnie sitting behind him. Donnie had gotten away from Julia, crawled on the cow dung floor, and sat there sucking his thumb!

After two years, our days at Mangwazane were coming to an end, but we had enjoyed hosting the many district meetings and missionaries who dared to travel the long, long driveway to visit us.

10

Trek Home As A Family

*W*hen due for furlough, we traveled to Durban to make travel arrangements. We were flying with a six-month-old baby and a boy who would turn two the day we would arrive in the States. We were assured that there would be enough baby food and disposable diapers on the plane.

We planned to drive to Vryheid, sell our car, and have our mission pilot, John Snavely, fly us to Jo'burg, to fly out the next day on Pam Am.

John strapped the two boys and me in the back seat of the Helio Courier, and Chuck sat in front. All went well, but bumpy, until we were within ten minutes of Jo'burg. We hit fog and an impeding storm so bad that John could not see the mountains well. He decided to turn back. I was not so disappointed in having to turn back, but I was nauseated from the bumpiness, plus keeping an eye on both children. Our return meant that our mission secretary drove us all the way to Jo'burg that afternoon, and we arrived late in the evening.

We got our flight the next day and were seated in the first row, with Ken in the wall bassinet. After a few hours, the stewardess said there was no more baby food or disposable diapers. The message had not been relayed!! They gave us their fine linen napkins for diapers. All Ken had for the entire trip was one jar of peaches, and two pabulums. It was good that I could supplement his need. This was also at the time of the Congo uprising. When we landed in Kinshasa, the plane parked at the end of the tarmac, and they shuttled people out to the plane by bus. One loud, inebriated man carried a large wooden curio and demanded that the stewardesses handle it very carefully.

Eventually, we settled in for a crowded trip, but the noise diminished enough to get "40 winks." Naturally, we arrived at JFK off schedule. A lady with a small child and we were the last ones to encounter Customs. (We had not been off the plane the whole trip of 10,000 miles.) We were told to go outside and catch a bus to another terminal for our connecting flight to Philadelphia. We had left South Africa wearing winter clothes and arrived in New York on June 2, one of the hottest days of the summer. We stood on the sidewalk and saw all the buses whizzing past us. One parked nearby, so Chuck asked the driver if that was the bus we were to take. The driver was sitting reading the newspaper, and he responded rather gruffly. We still didn't know where to go, and the buses kept whizzing past. Thinking the man didn't understand our destination, Chuck returned to his open window and asked again. Shouting obscenities, he pointed to an indefinite place, and said, "I told you, OVER THERE!!!" With the two children in my arms, and Chuck managing our suitcases, I said very dejectedly, "We're *home*."

Somehow, we managed to get to the proper terminal, only to find that we had missed our flight to Philadelphia. We waited and embarked on the next plane.

After we took off, and as soon as the "seat belt off" sign showed up, Chuck went back to freshen up, and I began to get the boys ready. Just as Chuck came back to us, the "fasten your seat belt" sign appeared. I had absolutely no time to freshen up. I was to meet his family and many people from his church for the first time. I was hot, tired, and felt very sloppy, to put it mildly. The expectant group had waited several hours for us, and I had to smile and greet them all. We finally reached Chuck's house and got introduced to others of the family. Later Chuck's father came home from work and gave me the biggest hug that made me feel a real part of the family.

11

Furlough — A Vacation?

*M*any not familiar with missionary service may think that a year's furlough is just a year of vacation. We do have times of relaxation, but that is not the whole story. One is constantly on call to balance fulfilling speaking obligations, caring for two very young children, lots of letter writing for speaking engagements (we had no computer or e-mail), scheduling all four of the family's full medical exams, keeping up with food preparations, washing and ironing, cleaning house, and most importantly — finding time for spiritual nourishment.

Our time was spent visiting churches in Michigan as well as in other states. Each conference came with its blessings and challenges. There was one particular conference known as a "Round Robin" conference, in the hills of West Virginia. This involved churches pooling their resources, thus enabling them to invite a number of missionaries to speak in all of the churches. Each missionary family stayed in one home, and then travelled and spoke in a different church each evening. The family with whom we stayed had two lovely young girls who spent all their time in their rooms playing with their dolls. We never heard a word from them!

You can imagine staying in a stranger's home with two very rambunctious boys, one ten months old and the other two-and- a-half years, for an entire week. Ken was just starting to stand and walk around the coffee table, which had a lovely vase in the middle. The lady just left it there and kept staring at him to see if he would dare to touch it. A day later, the husband said that if we desired, we could move to a motel and the church would pay for it, BUT we were welcome to stay with them. We knew these country churches had little in the way of finances, and we were hesitant to cause more expense. Several times, they gave us this option. After two days, we very reluctantly decided to take them up on their offer to stay at the motel.

Furlough is a most disorganized life. Often our home church would find a house for us to rent, and they would furnish it with the necessary furniture. We deeply appreciated their concern, but one would still get frustrated at not having one's favorite paring knife, and other familiar items we were so used to, which made our living easier. At the end of our furlough, we would then return all the borrowed items.

Visiting and staying in various homes provided us with special opportunities to go water skiing, tobogganing, being guests in nice restaurants, etc. The highlight of these visits was getting to know more closely the various people who were praying for us, as well as our relating God's marvelous work in the lives of some South Africans. It was a deep joy that kept us going, and increased our own burden for the ministry.

When our sons were young, we would divide our furlough time, spending six months in Michigan (my home area), and then six months in New Jersey (Chuck's home area). To make the move we rented a small U-Haul trailer to convey our few essential items we would need to live until our departure to South Africa. One time we got as far as entering the Pennsylvania Turnpike, but the toll collector would not allow us to continue with a trailer due to the high winds and blowing snow. So we had to go off the toll road and travel winding streets through all the small towns at 35 m.p.h. We had anticipated getting into Maple Shade, N.J., around 11:00 p.m. Instead, we reached our destination at 4:00 a.m. People had made our beds, so we just put the boys in their cribs, and we sank down into our welcome bed, totally exhausted after the normal 17-hour trip extended to 22 hours!!

The six months passed rather quickly, and we found ourselves buying and collecting necessary items to take back to South Africa. These we packed solidly in 45-gallon steel drums to be shipped ahead of us. These drums had a partial ring that snapped under a latch and allowed it to be locked with a padlock to prevent theft of the contents within the drum. Items we would need upon our arrival were packed in cardboard boxes, which could not exceed the Stateside 70 pounds in weight. We were each allowed one box, which went on the plane with us.

We tried to prepare our sons for the flight and the change to South Africa. Kenny was too young to understand, but Donnie could comprehend it. We had packed away a little plastic riding tractor he had been given, so we told him we were going to Mangwazana to get his "ugandaganda," the Zulu word he knew for "tractor."

12

Back To South Africa

"Workers together with Him"

CHUCK AND BEV   KENNY AND DONNIE

1969

Family prayer card

$\mathcal{T}$he time came for our departure, amidst all the tears, hugs, and goodbyes. We had an uneventful trip with a layover in London, England. We had lost six hours of sleep, so as soon as we got to the hotel, our heads hit the pillows rather quickly for a few hours. We did see the "Changing of the Guard" in front of Buckingham Palace. This was very impressive to our sons, and when we got settled in South Africa, they would march around our house drumming on their toy drums with their staccato strut.

Don and Ken after Buckingham Palace

Wanted: a Tractor

From London the next day we flew on to Durban, South Africa, where we were met by the McCallisters. They took us to Concord, a rest home for missionaries. We stayed a couple of days in Durban. After purchasing a car, Chuck took Donnie and went to Mangwazana to arrange for our stored items to be transferred to Dundee, the place of a new assignment. They stayed in the small town of Mkuzi at the bottom of the mountain. Early the next morning, Donnie woke up and said, "Daddy, can we go to South Africa and get my "ugandaganda." He had arrived!!

Don has arrived!!

Our New Home in Dundee

At Mangwazane, they loaded some stored items into the car, and travelled to Dundee. He had asked the neighbor lady if she would keep the key to let the movers place the things in the empty house. Then they travelled on down to Durban, approximately 300 miles to bring Kenny and me to our new home. It was a two-bedroom, plus a small office room, bathroom, kitchen, and an open dining-living room combination. It was an old house with wooden floors throughout. It had been built during the war. There was no basement, so it had just a very small space underneath the house with air bricks for ventilation. This seemed ideal, except that throughout the house the tongue and groove flooring had long gaps of missing wood; the effect of termites. This allowed cool air to come in. With Dundee being in the midlands, we had cold enough winters with frost, and even occasional light snow. As the cold weather approached, we had to buy a large rug for the bedroom and carpeting for the living room to somewhat eliminate the natural air conditioning. There was a corner fireplace in the living room, which we used, but being radiant heat, it didn't suffice for the rest of the house.

The kitchen was a12 x 12 square room, so Chuck bought three 4-x-12 Masonite boards to cover the weak and gapping floor, which also gave it a level and stable footing. The sink was a one-bowl type which left about three feet of counter to its right. The doors below, when opened, exposed half-logs as shelving and a bucket to collect the sink drain. On the opposite side of the room were two full-sized doors elevated on about a four-inch platform, which when opened, revealed narrow shelves. They were not wide enough to hold a plate.

More Renovations

Since Chuck had created two other kitchens for me in our short three-year marriage, I decided to just accept whatever I found and not ask him to build another kitchen. However, one evening while in the kitchen, he stood in the doorway and said, "Well, we can put the fridge over there, and the stove over here, and a new sink in there." I was amazed, but more so after he finished off the best kitchen I have ever had, with plenty of counter space to roll out pecan rolls, etc. The platform cupboard doors were removed and he made a fold-down table propped up with two wooden legs. The platform with chairs across from each other, served as high chairs for our sons. The table stuck out in the room, but it could be lifted up if something large had to be carried through the area. All this in a 12-foot- square room with three doors opening into the room made it a challenge to organize it.

<u>Dogs Attack</u>

Backing up a little in time, I experienced a trauma which left me with a life-long fear, still with me to this day.

After we were in the house only a few days, we got notice of our shipment having arrived in Durban. So Chuck took Donnie and went down to arrange for its consignment by rail to Dundee. He left in the morning and I got busy writing letters. Kenny played around in the almost empty house. I sensed he was getting restless, so I thought I would take him up the street to mail some letters. We went out our bush-lined, fenced yard toward our neighbor, whose driveway bordered ours, but was separated by a high wire fence. Our elderly neighbor was in the yard, and I wanted to meet and thank her for keeping the key for the movers. I was at the wire-fenced driveway gate, and her two large Rottweiler dogs were barking loudly, but it didn't alarm me. Above the noise she asked me to come inside the smaller front gate, which I approached with 21-month-old Kenny in my arms. However, as soon as she opened the gate, the dogs leaped out and one got hold of Kenny. I swung around with the thought that Kenny's arm was dangling. At the same time, the other dog got hold of me in the seat. I tried to hold Kenny as high as I could, but since I'm short, it was not very high. There was a gardener and the lady right there, but I think they were in too much in shock to get the dogs off from us immediately.

I was looking the dogs straight in their eyes as they jumped up and continued their attacks. It seemed like a very long time, but it probably was only about two or three minutes before they could get the dogs in their yard. My dress was torn, and I was crying and shaking like a leaf. The lady took Kenny in her arms and wanted to take him in the house to wash the wound with an antiseptic. I kept saying, "No, I'm a nurse. I'll take him home." I just wanted to get home. She kept insisting, so I conceded, and we walked toward the front door. Unbeknown to us, the gardener had put the dogs in the house, and as soon as she started to open the door, the dogs were pushing to get out. She then handed Kenny to me, and I quickly went home.

Chuck was not due back until late the next day, I had no car, nor a telephone, and I was NOT going outside our yard again. After a few hours, I saw the lady in her yard. Over the fence, I asked her if the dogs had their rabies shots, and she said "Yes." She was an Afrikaans speaking lady, and for some reason I asked her again, and again her answer was in the affirmative. Then I thought maybe she doesn't understand my American accent, so for the third time I repeated my concern. This time she said, "No." I had seen several tetanus deaths, and know the trauma they go through, so my concern rose to the heights. I went inside my house, not knowing what I could do. A little later she came to tell me her son was coming home earlier from work to take us to the doctor, which he did.

At the doctor's office, as he was probing the deep wound on Kenny's thigh, I asked if there was any danger of rabies. He answered very assuredly, "No. We haven't had a case of rabies for 18 months." I thought, "*18 months*?!" That didn't console me very much!!

We went home, and I made our supper, but I seemed unable to control my thoughts. I just kept thinking about what might happen to Kenny. I caught myself putting ice cream away in the unlit oven, and other nonsensical actions. I had no option but just to wait for Chuck and Donnie to arrive the next day. I had no way to notify them.

When Chuck arrived, he went to a phone booth in town and called our mission doctor at the hospital at Ingwavuma for advice. He suggested that we report it to the police, and have the local vet watch the dogs to see if rabies developed. If it happened within the time limit, both Kenny and I would have to undergo the 21 daily injections. He also said that if it went to the limit, then we would be in trouble. The perturbing fact was that the last day of the time limit would be the last day of our chance to begin the injections in order to obtain immunity. So all we could do was to rely on our Lord to do whatever He saw to be right. We also sent many letters to friends, whom we knew were praying for us. We watched and waited.

In our wait, one day we saw a salesman knock on our neighbor's door. The two dogs came running from behind the house, up on the porch, cornering him and attacking his legs. He was yelling and jumping up and down until the owner came and got the dogs under control and into the house. This was also reported to the proper authorities, and they then took the dogs for surveillance. What they did with them, we do not know, but God kept us safe, and we didn't get rabies. Most South African dogs are kept for protection, and therefore are usually strong and fierce.

There have been, through the years, other instances of near-attacks which have only worsened my deep-seated fear. I have had all kinds of advice and counseling, but unconsciously I emit a scent that dogs pick up, and they go for me. It is said dogs have a sense of smell 400 times that of a human being, of which I am acutely aware, and try to distance myself.

Continued Church Ministry

We continued on with our church planting ministry in the Dundee area, but even after repeated application for a church site on which to build an edifice for our two groups, we were constantly turned down. The reason stated was that all the church sites had already been allocated. When they plan out a township, they also plan on a certain amount of church sites, on a first-come basis. Since we were late, there was none left. So we continued to rent the Community Hall every Sunday, and supplied support to a two small groups a few miles from the city.

Behind our house on our property was a small building (about 8'x15') used by the previous tenants to raise rabbits, but it was very clean. Chuck used it for a while as his study.

It had a very low roof, which made it too hot for studying in the summer. Therefore, after a short time, he got the idea of using it for a bookstore to supply Zulu Bibles and vernacular books to the Africans. He built a few shelves and put linoleum on the floor. When we decided to have the opening day, our four-year-old Donnie saw a man walking in front of the house, and running out toward him, he called out saying, "Hey, Mister, come buy some books!" A new salesman in the making?

Chuck also built a portable book rack to put in the back of the station wagon. When the back door was raised, he could prop it up for people to see the titles. Once a month, he drove up to Newcastle, about 30 miles away, and sold books to the factory workers. He also placed some in the small African stores. He felt it imperative to get Bibles and biblical literature into the hands of the people, where there was no other source for them to obtain them.

Hunger for literature

Book rack in African store

It was also during our time in Dundee that Donnie, at four-and-a-half years of age, accepted Jesus as his Savior. One day Chuck had disciplined him, and he came in the house crying. I asked what was the matter and he told me. I comforted him and said that "Daddy has to discipline you if you do something wrong." Then we began to notice that he didn't want to pray before going to sleep, and other things that were not normal for him. We began to wonder if he was under conviction of sin. One day he came to me and asked, "Mommy, what is sin?" I put my arm around him and said, "Donnie, it is anything that Daddy does wrong, or Mommy does wrong, or Kenny does wrong, or you do wrong." With the last person mentioned, he just pulled away from me and said nothing more.

A week or so later, we were on vacation in Durban. Chuck had to return the 300 miles to Dundee to fulfill a previously arranged preaching commitment. He took Donnie with him, while Ken and I stayed in Durban. On the way, Donnie asked if he could preach! Chuck said that he had to be a Christian before he could preach. During the trip, Donnie asked to be saved. So he learned 1 John 4:19 in Zulu, and recited it before the congregation. When they arrived back the next day, the first thing he said to me was that he had accepted Jesus into his heart.

Children are a real joy! Kenny had a keen sense of humor. He didn't have to try to be funny, he just naturally was! One day both boys were in the small tree outside our kitchen window, but Kenny was above Donnie right at the very top. I happened to look out the window and seeing him, I meant to say "Come down," but I said, "Ken, don't go any higher" He turned his head in both directions, and said "I can't!" And it was true, he couldn't!

He did things that would take seven years off one's life. He would gleefully stand on the lowered rail of his bed.

A future acrobat!

How high can I go?

Donnie became concerned for Kenny's salvation. One evening I was reading to them about Jesus' return, when Donnie said, "When He comes I'm going to run and open the gate." I said, "But He is coming in the air." "Oh, I'll jump up to Him!" He turned to Kenny and said, "Don't you want to ask Jesus into your heart? While holding his favorite blanket and sucking his thumb, Ken's nonchalant answer was, "Nope, not tonight, tomorrow!" (In later years, he did profess Christ.)

Under apartheid, we had to live in the "white" area, and travel out to the "black" area for our ministry points. Thus, our sons spoke mostly English. As the boys got older, they didn't want to go to the Zulu services, because they didn't understand Zulu. So we decided that we would all go only to the big events, like Christmas and Easter. Otherwise I would teach them Sunday school at home. They were four and five at the time.

One Sunday, I was in bed and not feeling well. Donnie came to me and wanted to have Sunday school. I said that if he wanted it, he would have to teach it. He agreed, so he got out some flannel graph material, and we three went in the living room. Ken and I were the "audience," while Don stood in front and started "preaching." In the midst of it he asked if my "little boy would like to accept Jesus"? I looked straight ahead and said, "I don't know. You'll have to ask him." So he asked him, and Tim (we changed to make-believe names), responded positively. The "preacher" asked Tim to come and sit in the chair in front, which he did. Then the preacher said, "Now, we are going to have communion."

That took me by surprise. I didn't want them to take the meaning lightly, nor did I want to put down their desires of pleasing God. So I said, "You know we only do this in church, but I'll do it just this one time." They agreed. I went into the kitchen, but as I was preparing, I heard Donnie say to Ken, "You know that Jesus is the Son of God, He died on the cross, was buried and rose again, and you have to be saved.

Do you want to ask Jesus into your heart?' Ken responded positively and they both came to the kitchen. Don excitedly said, "Mom, Kenny just accepted the Lord." I turned to Ken and said, "Did you, Ken?" "Yep!" he said. And with that he turned a somersault. I thought, "You are not ready yet."

We also went out into the district surrounding Dundee and held Bible studies and church services, usually in huts, or in a small building Chuck had built. It was a joy to me as I taught a ladies' Bible class that one lady just broke down crying and said that she didn't want to live her old life anymore, and she became a Christian. I had never said anything about specific sin, etc. God's Spirit just convicted her of sin, even as we sat together on the cow dung floor, and with tears overflowing, she poured out her heart to God. I often think of Mina and still remember her.

Fruit amongst Farmers

A European friend asked me to go with her to her sister-in-law's farm who wanted to talk about the Lord. I agreed. It was outside of Glencoe, and Joy was waiting for us. As we got started, I just showed her in Ephesians 2:8, 9: "For by grace are ye saved through faith, and that not of yourself,

153

it is the gift of God — not of works, lest any man should boast." Before I had even finished the sentence, she said, "Nobody ever told me that it was a gift!" Her face lit up and she still bears the light. In 1999, we visited her in South Africa and her face still glowed with joy and confidence in Him. It was a time of much crime and unrest in the country. As we walked with her into her house, I noticed that there were no dogs, and she said, "Oh, they just poison them." Knowing the crime that was rampantly reported, I asked, "Aren't you afraid living out here alone?" With her face glowing, she looked at me and replied, "No. I'm not alone. The Lord is with me."

13

Empangeni — The Third Trek

We were unable to obtain a church site, since all were previously taken before we moved to Dundee, so when our furlough was due, the mission decided that we should return to a new area of Natal, South Africa. The government was building a new harbor at Richards Bay and two huge townships were being established.

There was a large amount of logging in this area, which made traveling the North Coast roads a little dangerous. The large logs would be piled high on the back of an open truck, only tied down lightly, or trusting wooden staves in the sides of the truck's bed to hold them. Many times one would roll off. One man had a log roll off and it came through his windscreen. It was especially hard at night, because drivers often would not turn on their lights. They thought that as long as they could see you coming, you should be able to see them!

Ministry Areas

Church Planting Beginnings

*U*pon our return from furlough in 1972, we went directly to the fairly new European town of Empangeni. Since the mission had no house there, they rented one for us. One was being built on the plot of sugar cane land they had purchased. They gave us the freedom to design the house with their cost approval. After six months, we moved into a brand new house, in which once again Chuck built all the cupboards — kitchen and bedrooms — to lower the costs. In the meantime, Chuck also began to make contacts in the two large townships of Esikhaweni and Ngwelezane. It wasn't long before there was a small group in both places, meeting in small township houses. We were surprised that several people who had been at our hospital at Ingwavuma and were now living in the city joined us. Soon, the small house could not contain all the people, so Chuck got permission to build a larger pastor's house at Esikhaweni with a large living room. The pastor and his family moved in, but soon the room became too small. So the plan for a large church was drawn up, and it was built.

Church Building

Slatted garage church

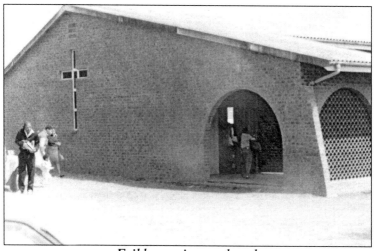

Esikhaweni new church

The other township, Ngwelezane, was old and small. So the government added a large extension. Right away Chuck applied for one of the allocated church sites, and after a time, his choice was granted. Again, at Ngwelezane, the church outgrew the tiny living room, so the owner built a part onto his house with wooden slats and a sheet iron roof to accommodate about 20 short backless wooden benches. Not long after, we were packed in like sardines. The slanting roof was only about six feet high. The separated wooden side slates let in a little air. Even with 80 people almost crushing one another in 100-120 degree heat and the services lasting two or more hours, the church still grew. The Esikhaweni church was still growing and doing well with a good pastor, so Chuck drew his attention to building another large church at

Ngwelezane. His permission from the mission was granted, so another fund raising project began, which put a lot of pressure on us to trust our Lord. And true to His name as the Provider, He did supply. In His time, another large brick church was erected. At the time of our leaving South Africa in 1991 to transfer to Czechoslovakia, there were about 250 in attendance. Since that time, they have had to extend the building another 20 x 40 feet.

As I have mentioned, the Zulus love to sing, and they have perfect pitch. So before the actual sermon is preached there is about an hour of singing. Different groups write their title on a scrape piece of paper and one will walk up to the emcee and make known their desire to participate. Then he calls them up front as their turn comes up. Even very small children will participate. It is all spontaneous. If they make a mistake or do not sing very well, the audience will clap their hands, and ooh and ah over them anyway. They will never make fun of them.

New Ministry Opportunity

In 1976, another opportunity opened up which we loved. We had always been involved with literature, and our mission wanted us to keep a lookout for renting a vacant store for selling books in the "white" city of Empangeni. There was very little Zulu literature, and there was no other way they could get books. Many could read English, so they also bought English books. There was an ideally situated empty store in town in the direct footpath of Africans going shopping. Chuck went to the business owners to rent it, but they just kept giving him excuses. Then a lady with a décor shop rented it, and our hearts sank. Chuck kept going past it, and one day he saw a "for let" sign in the window. Immediately, he inquired if she wanted to go out. With her yes answer, he phoned immediately to a friend in Durban, who had a friend in the same company, and who was over the one in Empangeni. He told them that they should let us rent it. He did.

We knew one of TEAM's bookstores in Jo'burg was going out of business because of a change in foot traffic. So we were able to obtain bookshelves, racks, and an initial stock of books transported to us. If we had obtained the facility when we had wanted it, we would have had to build shelves, order books, etc., in order to open the store. God knew the timing. **"God may delay, but He is never late!"**

TEAM book store

The first week of the store's opening, we gave away Hal Lindsey's book, *The Late Great Planet Earth* to everyone. One sailor, whose ship was docked at Richards Bay, received it. He came back three months later and said that they had gone around the world, and everyone on the ship had read it. The extension ministry of the smallest bookstore in South Africa encircled the world!

We learned a new lesson of faith. We could not go out and invite people to come and buy, but had to patiently wait for God to send them in to us. In order to meet expenses, we calculated we had to sell an average of 40 rand (about $35.00) a day. An old hand-cranked sales slip machine was given to us. In order to cut expenses, we would even roll the paper over and print on the back side. As the ministry of the store grew, we were able to get a modern cash register, more books, racks, and music. It was not long before we became well known to the various churches to supply their needs in terms of song books, children's ministry material, and adult Bible studies. God gave us opportunity for sensing the spiritual pulse of the churches, in order to recommend books and material to the people. About the same time, there was a very real spiritual awaking, mainly in two of the churches.

The store was staffed by either Chuck or me, and one of our African ladies. We both had other previous commitments of Bible studies, church ministries, etc., so neither of us was in the store at the same time, except at very busy seasons like Christmas and Easter. Chuck would always relieve me at 3:00 p.m. in order for me to fetch the children from school, help them with their school work, and make our supper. After the children were in bed, I would scan through several books in order to know how to recommend them to various customers. It was very tiring, but so spiritually rewarding.

Furlough after eight years

We were due for our furlough about the same time as he finished building the last church. After EIGHT years without being home, we once again packed our earthly belongings into 45-gallon drums and left them in storage. We left in the morning to pick up our sons from Treverton high school's matriculation service, where Don completed his schooling. We left there, drove directly to Jan Smuts Airport, and flew out to the U.S.A.

We knew we would have to be home longer than the normal year furlough. This was necessary so that Ken could finish high school in the States. In S. A., in order to graduate, every student has to take and pass a government exam, which covers the last two years of school. These exams are all taken at the same time in every school all over the country. There are no excuses, for headaches, sickness, or whatever. If we were to take Ken back at the end of the year, he already would have missed a whole year. So along with the mission, we decided that we would stay home for three years. The S.A. school year begins with the month of January, which lengthened the time involved. Don entered college, and Ken began his last two years of high school in Grand Rapids.

God's Provision in the States

We landed in New Jersey to visit Chuck's family for a week, and then traveled by car to Grand Rapids, Michigan. In the meantime, our Rockford church was trying to locate a house for us to rent, but to no avail. However, one family was going to Haiti to visit their missionary family, and they said that we could stay in their house for the ten days they would be gone. We were so grateful. Chuck took both boys to enroll in schools in Grand Rapids, and he also wanted to get more seminary training. As he spoke with the Dean of Admissions at Cornerstone University, he was asked where he was living, and Chuck explained the situation. The Dean told him that his church had a house for missionaries on furlough, and it was empty. The Dean could have waited to talk with the committee later, but he picked up the phone immediately and made arrangements that we could use it. Since we were not missionaries from that church, we were allowed to use it for six months at a time unless one of their own missionaries needed it. So we moved into the missionary house two days before the family was due home from Haiti. God's timing is amazing!!

Leaving Our Sons in the States

In thinking ahead, we began to realize after our return to South Africa we would need to make housing arrangements for our two sons, for the time when they were out of college in the summer. So Chuck began to count the cost of building a house. He was away for two weeks, and I began to read the newspapers for land for sale. I found one ad for ten acres. We had talked about a couple of acres to plant some fruit trees and to have a small garden, but NOT *ten acres!* However, it was just two miles outside of Rockford, where our church was located and where we did most of our shopping. It seemed an ideal location. I called the realtor and said that since my husband was away, I could not make a decision, nor did I want to be hassled with telephone calls. She agreed. When Chuck arrived home, I told him about it and we went to see its location. Next, he called the realtor and got more specifics, as to the price and such. The price seemed astronomical to us; when we began to count up our savings, insurance policies, etc., we came short by about $2,000. The realtor didn't think that the owner would accept our offer. We told him that we were not trying to shortchange him, but that that was all we had. To the surprise of us all he accepted it. We later found out that the land was once looked at by a developer, but he relinquished it. Another lady wanted it for her horse, but the grass was not suitable for the horse. So God held it those three months for us!

Now, we had to start building, but that takes money, too. If Chuck had to build, I had to find a job. Since we had done some proofreading for the Zulu Concordance, I thought of doing that. However, they told me it would take three months to be trained in the American method, and we needed the money NOW. A friend told me about a position at the nursing home where she worked in Grand Rapids. I kept saying that I had been out of nursing for 22 years, was not up on meds, etc., but she insisted that I could do it. Finally, I went for an interview with the Director of Nursing. She asked if I still had a valid nurse's license. I had to say that I had cancelled it, since I could not use it in South Africa. Right away, she called the Nurses' Association in Lansing, and they said as long as I had my original license number, I could be reinstated. The Director was a little shocked, but she hired me. The other nurses were so very helpful in my orientation.

We had one car, which was all right, but when school began, both sons and Chuck were going to school in Grand

Rapids in the daytime; I had to go on the 11 p.m.-7 a.m. shift, which I really preferred. By the time I drove the 35 miles each way and bought gas, I was clearing about only $3.75 an hour. I knew I could not work at a hospital, where the pay would be much higher, so I had to be content. Then a dispute came up with a new Director, and nurses who had been there for 15 or 20 years were quitting. I felt that, in spite of the low pay, they had been good enough to hire me and tolerate me, and I could not leave. Also, the Director seemed to accept me, even to the point of asking my advice. She would say, "Bev, you always you tell me the truth." I also felt that I should stay to witness to her.

However, my friend Lorna, who had gotten me back into nursing, was one of those who had quit and gone to Veteran's Hospital. She often would call and say, "Bev, why don't you come over to Vet's. It is so much better, with better pay." I kept saying, "No, I think I should stay here." Then one afternoon, after I woke up from working nights, my first thought was, "Vet's! Why not?" I immediately went to the phone and asked if they had any openings for a R.N. The person said, "Just a moment." I thought he was going to look on a list, but he put me through to the Director of Nurses, who made an appointment for me to meet with her. She realized that I had been out of nursing for a long period and asked why. I told her I had been on the mission field. She then asked if I was going back again, and when. I told her that we still had to do deputation, and it might not be until five months. She then asked me if I had any questions. We had a two-week deputation trip already scheduled. Chuck had said that under no circumstances could we forfeit it. I told her, and to my surprise, she looked over to her assistant and said, "I don't think that is a problem. Do you?" Of course, she almost had to agree. So we see God is even in the planning!

I had two weeks of orientation, went on our two weeks of meetings, and then started working. The other nurses often said, "Bev, they just do not hire a nurse for five months!" BUT GOD WORKS! At the Nursing Home, as well as at Vet's, I worked holidays and double shifts as much as possible, in order to earn more money. I would bring home the paycheck, and Chuck would go to the lumber company, buy the wood, load it on the top of the car, drive up to the lot, and build all day. By that time, Don had his own car, and the two boys went to school together. I still had to keep up with the housework and meals and catch as much sleep as possible, but I was really getting very worn out.

A situation arose at the missionary home where we were living that necessitated us leaving earlier than we had anticipated. We began to look for alternative housing, but found nothing. Little did we know: God had it all planned out.

At the time, I was attending a ladies' Bible Study group, and when prayer requests were made, I explained our situation with a steady stream of tears flowing down my cheeks. One lady spoke up and said that her mother was going into a nursing home, and we could stay there until something else came up. Of course, it happened that Chuck was gone on meetings again, so I packed our bedding and our eating utensils in boxes. My sister Charlene came and transported me to Grand Rapids, to another very temporary living situation. We arrived and found a padlock on the door. We waited, and finally a car pulled up across the street. Thinking it was the lady's husband to unlock the door, I asked him, and his reply was, "No, I'm the realtor. This home is up for sale, and I will be bringing people through it." Even in tough situations, God give us a sense of humor. My shocked reply was, "But there are just boxes piled in the kitchen!"

The house was empty except for two cots in the bedroom. I had to put a "night nurse sleeping" sign on the bedroom door, in hopes that no one would disturb me. Don and

Ken had to sleep on the living room floor at night, and it was during their exam time. They never complained.

Then, just in time for us to be out of the house, another lady said that someone in her church was going to Florida and wanted to rent out their house for the winter. We went for an interview, and out of five others, they rented it to us. It was just a mile away from where we were staying at the time, and it would be just a mile closer to where I was working nights. God had the most detailed plans all worked out for our benefit.

Chuck had just finished building our house in Rockford at the same time the family was due to come back from Florida. Once again, we moved our boxes to our own home. We were extremely thankful to our God.

I must tell about another amazing incident that happened a little before our having to leave the missionary house. We knew we would not be able to build on the small wages I was receiving. Previously three people who had heard of our building intentions had said that if we needed help, maybe they could loan us some money. When it was time, though, we asked them, but for one reason or another, they could not. We understood. After that, I can remember praying, "Lord, you **send** someone to us who will give us an interest-free loan!!" I had never thought that, and I prayed it once and left it never to pray it again. It had come into my thoughts only once and went out again.

About three months later, we had invited a couple over for dinner. I was in the kitchen, putting the finishing touches on the meal, and the lady was sitting in the kitchen also. She said, "Bev, what are you folks doing now?" I replied, "We are starting to build." Without hesitation, Pat said, "If you need help, we can give you an interest-free loan." I was stirring the gravy, and I turned around very astonished, and said, "Those are the exact words that I prayed!" Chuck and I talked it over, and agreed to it. God **is** our Provider!

Don was in college, and after high school graduation, Ken enrolled in the same college. They both seemed content, so we made final preparations for our return to South Africa.

PART TWO

1

The Trek To Czechoslovakia

Calling to Czechoslovakia

*W*hile Chuck was still building the last large brick church at Ngwelezane, he came home one day and said, "Bev, I think we need a change." I looked at him, and seeing his loss of weight (at five foot eight, he now weighed only 117 pounds), I thought he was just tired. Neither of us said anything more about it. Then he came home a couple of days later, and said the same thing. I really took notice then, and started thinking, "We are in the height of our ministry. We have so many friends in this community — both black and white, and they know us!" We began talking about it together. Where could we go in South Africa and still use our

175

Zulu language? We pondered it a lot, but could not come up with any other place. Yet, Chuck kept sensing the Holy Spirit prompting him to move, but to where?

While on furlough, we attended our annual conference, where different missionaries would tell how God was working in their area. One told about the Berlin Wall coming down, and the open doors of opportunity. Chuck said right away, "That's it!!" At long last, God had definitely shown him what the Holy Spirit was nudging him to do. He talked with our director and received approval to go back to South Africa, in order to terminate our part in the ministry there, and to "*valelisa*" (say goodbye) to the many African friends and churches. We thought we would go to Eastern Germany, so we began to study German via tapes. However, they decided we should go to Czechoslovakia along with a single short-term missionary. We concurred, and began to search information on this new development. We tried to gather facts on the country, but with South Africa's dislike for Communism, we found nothing in the library. So, we had to go to Czechoslovakia only with God's leading.

Return to Zululand for Final Farewells

It was interesting how the Africans accepted it. They compared us to Abraham and Sarah as to going out from Haran, not knowing where they were going. Or, were they comparing us to Abraham's and Sarah's ages?! After all, we were nearing retirement age!

Before leaving S.A. for our transfer to Czechoslovakia, we went to all the churches in Zululand to "*valelisa*," to say goodbye. This is customary, and not to do so would mean that you never left S.A. They often gave gifts of grass — woven dishes, straw mats, etc. However, at one of the country churches, they gave me (not Chuck) a LIVE goat. I kept insisting that I could not keep a goat in the "white" city yard with no fencing and neighbors all around. They insisted just as strongly that I should take it. So we finally loaded it in the back of our pickup, and on the way, dropped it off at another country pastor's home. They used it to feed people who attended special meetings there several weeks later.

Between saying goodbyes, we began sorting out our household goods. We had to decide what to sell, give away, or ship to Prague. The first time through the house, I decided what I could get along without. The second time through, I decided what I really would not need. The third time through, I decided what I would really need. Not knowing what we could expect, we watched TV for clues as to housing, clothes to wear, etc. We wanted to fit in with the people and culture. We ended up taking four boxes that included our bedding, sheets, pillows, four plastic plates, tableware, a couple pots, and a few books and clothes. When we got to Prague, I found that God had really directed in my choices. We got along with that until a few more items reached us nine months later.

Things We Learned

Zulus are very clever. If a child is outside during school hours, a policeman will put the child's arm over its one ear and head to see if the child can touch the other ear. If so, they are six years old and should be in school.

In Dundee, we had three huge double-forked pine trees, from which the large pine cones would drop — sometimes, on our heads. We had a local man recommended to us who could cut them down. So we hired him. It was very tricky, because the trunks had to land between our house, the small bookstore building, and our neighbor's garage. The African man would walk out from the tree trunk, stop, and look between his legs until he saw the top of the tree, making it a triangle. That is where it would fall. It happened every time, without any damage to the buildings around. It was a perfect geometry lesson.

We feel so very privileged to have been a part of God's ministry in that area, as well as in other parts of South Africa. Our sons, born and raised in South Africa, also have a great affinity for that country.

2

<u>The Cobblestone Streets Of Prague</u>

Prague--Charles Bridge and castle

*W*e were going into the country two years after the fall of Communism, and many of the effects were still very evident.

We were very pleasantly surprised when we met with the Czech pastor and his wife, and they took us to our apartment. One of their church members rented it to us for six months. It was sparsely, but adequately furnished. There were even some food items in the cupboard. Their thoughtfulness was much appreciated and unexpected. All the apartments are called panelects, because they are cement panels moved into place by cranes. They dominated the neighborhood and the entire skyline. Some apartments are only four stories high, but most of them are 12-14 stories high. The high-rise apartments were designed all the same inside. When we had to move to another apartment, I knew exactly where to put my towels, kitchen utensils, and everything. In our second move, God gave us a very honest owner. He left a couch, kitchen table with two chairs, a stove, and refrigerator, as well as a small wardrobe. He charged us only the basic rent and gave us all the keys to the apartment. Most other landlords charged much more and kept one key to the apartment, whereby they could enter anytime.

Shopping and Adjustments

We left S.A. in the heat of summer and with no real winter clothes. We arrived in Prague in the middle of winter. Shopping was a new experience. We had to walk two blocks to get the bus to go into town to larger stores. No plastic bags were supplied for one to carry home their purchases, so one had to buy something in which to carry the items. Eggs were sold in a small paper bag, not in an egg carton. We gingerly carried them home, hoping that none got cracked during the transportation coming home. We had to walk the ten minutes to our apartment, with the constant cold wintery wind blowing. We had no gloves; it was very cold. We tried to buy gloves as our Christmas present to each other. In the store, all goods were neatly stacked in cubby holes behind the counter. You would point to an object, and the clerk would let you see it. Even if you wanted to buy a sweater, you would stand in line, wait your turn, and point to a sweater neatly folded up on a shelf behind the clerk. She would take it down and hold it up to see if you agreed to the size. If not the right one, she would fold it again, and put it back on the shelf She repeated this, until you decided on the right one. All this time, people are queuing up behind you. Patience!

To buy toilet tissue, you didn't go to the grocery section, but to a separate stationery store.

In every store, you waited in line for an empty trolley, or a small handheld plastic basket which was not large enough to hold anything much. Its purpose was to control how many people were in the store itself. There were no packages of meat. Everyone stood in line with their little carts in front of them, waiting their turn to have the butcher grant their request. That could take anywhere from 20 to 30 minutes.

In the little store in our neighborhood, milk was sold in liter-size plastic bags. Most of these would leak a few drops at a time, which made them very sticky and less than a liter. A friend took us to the little store to teach us what some things were and what was available. However, an authoritative-looking lady followed us around the whole time we were there. Even the labels on cans of peas, etc. were printed with the price and it didn't change. It was stable. There was no free market, so prices were always the same. The government was sure that their reign would be secure.

Life under Communism

One of the hardest things people had to endure was that those who owned houses or apartments were told by the authorities that they didn't need all their rooms or apartments. If a house was built for generational families, the government would move other people in. However, now that there is a law for the original owners to reclaim their domains, how does one get the people (usually very old by now) to vacate the premises after 40 years of living there? They are poor, and have no place to go. Such are some of the results of crumbled socialized Communism.

With the downfall, a new government had to be formed, with all new laws and such. This often was very confusing to ones who had lived 40 years under that regime. The stores were reorganized so that people were free to go anywhere in the store without even a basket. They could pick up things and look at them. This was confusing to the clerks, who had controlled everything before. One clerk said, "They just go everywhere, even behind the counter, and touch anything!"

The educational system is very advanced. Eight- and nine-year-old boys were learning about amperes, and voltage, etc. We had several scientists and PhDs in our small church, but they were so humble no one would not know it.

English Classes

We entered under the auspices of a Czech church and used English as a contact with the people. Teaching English helped us to reach many Czechs who didn't use English in their everyday life and were not Christians.

We enrolled in a total immersion course taught at the Berlitz School of languages. Czech is a language that relies on very specific grammar and pronunciation to communicate.

Now that the people were free, they wanted to learn English to enable them to get better jobs there and in the surrounding countries. So we began advertising our lessons as "Learn English by studying the Bible." We started out with about ten students — mostly university students and a few adults. In no time at all, the unsaved students were inviting their unsaved friends, until there were about 23 in attendance. Their background stories were amazing.

English class students

One university student came and declared he was an atheist, but he soon gravitated to Chuck. As time went on, he invited Chuck to his parents' home in the mountains for the weekend. His mother had made apple *zaven* — like apple pie — and Chuck made the comment that it was his favorite. She then made it for him every day he was there. This student took Chuck hiking every day and showed him all the different things in the fields. It was quite a biology lesson!! The best thing was when this student said, "I didn't believe there is a God, but now I do believe there is one, even though I cannot see how He can be an influence in my life."

A Son Returns

One lady, Vlasta, was in a bad auto accident in 1968 and hospitalized for a long time. Only later did she learn that her husband had taken her two children to his mother's, and then on to America. After her discharge from the hospital, the government let her travel to America to attend a court case to try to get them back. She was under restrictions all the time that she was in America. Finally, the judge refused their return to a Communist country, so she returned without them, and with a very heavy heart.

She tried to keep up contact with them by mail, but that waned after a time, and all contact was lost. She did receive a high school graduation invitation from her son years later. She asked us if we could try contacting him through the school. Chuck took the challenge, and through a neighbor in America who remembered the children, he obtained an address of the son's possible present residence. Through trial and error, we finally made contact, and she talked with her son, Fritz, for the first time in about 32 years.

Her English was not so good, and Fritz didn't remember Czech, so the conversation was not without misunderstandings! He had said that he would come to Prague, and she thought it would be very soon, like the next week. So we had to explain to her that he would come, but after a time. In a few months, he did come. We were at the airport with her. As we watched her seeing his plane land, you could almost imagine the thoughts that were running through her mind. What did he look like? How would he be? Would he accept her? So many thoughts were evident.

Vlasta and son, Fritz

As soon as Fritz got through passport control, he didn't wait to go through customs. When he saw her, he ran up the stairs, hugged her tightly, and said, "Hi, Mom!" It caused tears to come to my eyes. He didn't hold anything against her for all that had happened. It was wonderful to have had a small part in their reunion. We didn't have the same success with her daughter. Vlasta still has not seen her. The son later married a girl in the Netherlands, and they live there with their children. So there is opportunity for each other to visit and to see the grandchildren.

3

The Long Trek Ends

*W*e lived in Prague for only eight and a half years and saw only one follow Christ for salvation. However, we answered their many questions about the Bible and saw their hunger. We can only try to keep in touch with some of them, and trust God to put someone else in our place to help them to understand. We have to recognize their difficulty of accepting another "ism" (even Christianity) after living under Communism for 40 years, when they were taught that "God is dead!" As one in the church said, "If God is dead, why do we fight against Him?"

The wonderful news is that after our leaving, another colleague and his family have been instrumental in starting three churches in Prague. Others are also being used to harvest ripe fruit. God is at work, even in the most atheistic country of Europe. The country peacefully divided with Slovakia in 1993, so now it is called the Czech Republic.

There is so must more I could relate, but this book would be so thick it could not contain it all. May it redound to His honor and glory, and to you a Christian benefit.

It has been an exciting 44 years for me (38 years for Chuck), and if we had it to do over, we would not hesitate. We learned so much about our God.

THE LONG TREK

From the winding paths of Zululand
to the cobblestone streets of Prague.

*C*ome, travel with me along the winding dusty roads of Zululand, a land rich in beauty, whose language (*isi-Zulu*) can be translated *heaven*. On the winding paths my life intersected with Africans in many areas. Some were people who lay recuperating from an illness. Some were members of a class of nurses; some I met along winding roads as I went to their church services. Sometimes, I was providing assurance at a *kraal*, where I came to see someone who needed transport to the hospital. Later, the winding roads led to a large city and sitting in churches not made of mud, but out of brick. After 36 years of our traveling the winding roads of Zululand, God led us to the cobblestone streets of Prague, where we sojourned for eight years.

We switched from a pickup truck, to no car at all, to traveling on an underground metro system (no dust!), buses, and trams. However, the purpose for living in Prague remained the same: to reach people with the gospel.

Chuck & Bev ministered overseas with The Evangelical Alliance Mission (TEAM) for a total period of 44 years.

CPSIA information can be obtained at www.ICGtesting.com
Printed in the USA
BVOW080108111212

307825BV00005B/10/P